To the
Queen of Creative
thinking!

Carla ¨

RE:Think Innovation

Praise for *RE:Think Innovation*

"Innovation is hard to define and even harder to execute. In plain English, Carla Johnson spells out exactly what it takes to reliably come up with great ideas. Even more crucially, RE:Think Innovation *presents a roadmap for implementing new ideas in large organizations. Candid, insightful, entertaining, and vivid, this book is an indispensable read for forward-thinking leaders."*

—**Dhiraj Mukherjee**, speaker, advisor, investor, and co-founder of Shazam

"Innovation is a word that's bandied around so much these days that it can be paralyzing to be expected to innovate in whatever context. Carla Johnson has written a terrific manual that brings much-needed simplicity, straightforwardness, and common sense to a step-by-step process guaranteed to spark the desired outcome—new, great, and reliable ideas. Highly recommended for anyone in need of a fresh perspective and inspiring stimulus to unleash their inner innovator."

—**Cindy Gallop**, founder & CEO of MakeLoveNotPorn

This book is an engaging guide that is chock-full of real-world examples for how to "do" innovation and create a sustainable innovation culture. Carla's simple but powerful five-step innovation framework is easy to remember and can be fully implemented with nothing more than a stack of colored Post-it notes. I am already applying her technique to generate new ideas for commercial applications of our research and to surface opportunities for improvements in our long-established technology transfer process. I know of no other book that will make an innovation mindset operational in your workplace as easily as RE: Think Innovation.

—**Jim Roberts**, technology licensing officer, MIT

"Smart people and successful companies consistently miss opportunity. With RE:Think Innovation, *Carla Johnson teaches you how to have more control over future success and your own creative potential.*"

—**Jeremy Gutsche**, CEO of Trend Hunter, *New York Times* bestselling author of *Better and Faster*, *Create the Future*, and *Exploiting Chaos*

"*Most innovation today is mere iteration, not true innovation at all. If you have a business to run, how do you break your own mold, become the industry pacesetter, grab market share, and at the same time keep your current customers happy and satisfied? This maneuver is akin to changing a tire on a moving vehicle, and Carla shows you how to do exactly that! If you're tired of talking about innovation and ready to truly stand out, this is your very next "must-read" business book.*"

—**Tamara McCleary**, futurist and CEO, Thulium.co

"*In today's business world, people need to find their own area of expertise and future-proof their career. For anyone who wants to be recognized as an innovator, Carla Johnson lays out the exact process for how to become the 'idea' person in any organization.* RE:Think Innovation *not only teaches a repeatable, scalable process for coming up with ideas, it also paves the way for creating a more innovative culture.*"

—**Dorie Clark**, author of *Entrepreneurial You* and executive education faculty, Duke University Fuqua School of Business

"*Carla Johnson is a recognized expert in business strategy and marketing. In this book she applies both those disciplines to business innovation. She presents a clear and concise formula not only for leaders who have innovation ideas for their organizations but, just as importantly, how to sell ideas for radical change up and down the organization: to peers, colleagues, the board, and the boss. Want to make change happen? This book is your roadmap.*"

—**Rebecca Lieb**, author, advisor, analyst

"I have a shelf of books on the topic of sustainable innovation. On the left side, I have The Innovator's Dilemma *by Harvard professor Clayton Christensen, in which he explains why innovation is so hard to sustain and harder to catch than a fish. On the other, I have the legendary Sir David Ogilvy and his book* Ogilvy on Advertising, *which explains how he grew a small ad firm into a global multinational company by using research and sustained creativity. Well, Carla Johnson's book is in the middle. And she took the best of both worlds—the chutzpah from Ogilvy and the deep analysis of what is sustainable innovation and how to do it. Will use in my classroom."*

—**José Berengueres**, PhD, professor of design thinking, University of Dubai, angel investor, and author of *Data Visualization and Storytelling*

"RE:Think Innovation breaks the myth that innovation is solely about big ideas. It's also about the people behind them and the culture in which they thrive. Carla Johnson brings all three together as she shows how teaching everyone in an organization innovative thinking leads to greater trust, better work, and phenomenal results."

—**Eduardo Conrado**, executive vice president and chief strategy and innovation officer, Ascension

"Nailed it! This is the spark your team needs to develop innovative human leaders inside any business at any level. Carla obviously poured herself into this book and created a masterpiece and formula for what, how, why, and when to create the innovation every company needs. This book will be sitting on my nightstand."

—**Bryan Kramer**, *USA Today* bestselling author of *H2H: Human-to-Human*, business coach, keynote speaker

"Stop! Before you gather the team for another brainstorming session, read this book! Carla's rich storytelling and simple, no-nonsense framework for building a culture of original thinkers is genius!"

—**Andrew Davis**, bestselling author

"RE:Think Innovation *gives practical lessons and makes innovation accessible to business leaders at any level. Many feel groundbreaking ideas happen only within notable brands, but the valuable gift Carla Johnson gives readers is a way to turn inspiration into action and ultimately create innovation in our everyday work. It's not our ideas that stop us, but how we execute, get leadership buy-in, and build them to last. A must-read that's equal parts practical and provocative for those trying to break through the noise and create something extraordinary."*

—**Amisha Gandhi**, marketing and communications executive, SAP

"Many companies talk about innovation but execute it in a limited fashion. Carla Johnson shows that success means looking at the entire organizational ecosystem of how new ideas get introduced, who's involved, and expectations about outcomes. For anyone wanting to become a core contributor to innovation, or lead their teams with more clarity or greater alignment, RE:Think Innovation *is the standard to follow."*

—**Jeremiah Owyang**, founding partner, Kaleido Insights

"This book lays out a step-by-step process for any person or company looking to innovate and achieve long-term differentiation. I love that it addresses pitching your idea, as that is where many ideas fall short—getting others to believe in it. This book is a must-read for executives, team leaders, and individuals looking to increase their idea generation and implementation."

—**Dr. Karen Bartuch**, marketing executive; adjunct professor, DePaul University; podcast host

RE:Think
INNOVATION

How the world's most prolific innovators
come up with great ideas that
deliver extraordinary outcomes.

Carla Johnson

NEW YORK

LONDON • NASHVILLE • MELBOURNE • VANCOUVER

RE:Think Innovation

How the World's Most Prolific Innovators Come Up with Great Ideas that Deliver Extraordinary Outcomes

PERPETUAL INNOVATION PROCESS is a trademark of Carla Johnson Productions

Published in New York, New York, by Morgan James Publishing. Morgan James is a trademark of Morgan James, LLC. www.MorganJamesPublishing.com

ISBN 9781631953170 paperback
ISBN 9781631953187 ebook
Library of Congress Control Number: 2020945527

Cover Design by:
Joseph Kalinowski and
Marcie Hancock

Interior Design by:
Christopher Kirk
www.GFSstudio.com

Morgan James is a proud partner of Habitat for Humanity Peninsula and Greater Williamsburg. Partners in building since 2006.

Get involved today! Visit
MorganJamesPublishing.com/giving-back

To Ron, Mel, Abby, and Nick,
who inspire me to rethink life, love,
and the meaning of the universe.
I'm deeply grateful for the extraordinary life you've given me.

Contents

Foreword

The "I" in *Innovation* Represents You and the Ideas You Contribute to Make a Dent in the Universe

"Imagination is the beginning of creation. You imagine what you desire, you will what you imagine, and at last, you create what you will."

—George Bernard Shaw

I *have an idea!*

This is something we need to hear more of these days. Ideas are the beginning of new possibilities. And new possibilities bring about new outcomes.

The thing about ideas is that everyone has them, but not everyone believes their ideas are worth considering. The truth is that we all have a vision for a brighter future, but not all of us have the confidence or support network to believe that what we think matters beyond our day-to-day roles in life and work. Yet, without having ideas and bringing them to life, we would not change the world—or anything, for that matter.

There's an old saying: The more things change, the more they stay the same. While it's natural to hold on to what we know, to protect customs and traditions, we cannot hold back progress or contain transformation or innovation, nor should we even try.

I get it. Comfort zones are safety nets. They can also be our happy place. There's something about our comfort zone that is not only familiar but also safeguarding. It's normal to appreciate where you are, what you have, and who you're with.

Gratitude is a superpower. So is the ability to change.

We can't ever assume that we've learned all that's necessary, accomplished all we can do, helped everyone in need, fixed everything that was broken, or discovered everything that makes this world and life so magical.

Navigating life as if our comfort zone is our center of reference, as if it will last forever and is without worry or consequence, is restrictive and cheats ourselves out of unleashing our potential. It keeps us stationary while the world evolves away from us. And not only is life evolving, but extraordinary transformation and disruption are accelerating. Everything we know and do is being challenged, pushed forward, built upon, or circumvented.

If 2020 has taught us anything, it's that disruption is as sweeping as it is inevitable. We learned that there are two types of responses: one being acceptance and driving resilience, and the other being denial and fighting for status quo. Which one do you think will thrive in the longer term?

This is our reality. But it doesn't mean that evolution and disruption are always disadvantageous. It's matter of attitude, really.

A pessimist will see challenges and obstructions. An optimist will see opportunities and new chances for different paths forward. It's like that old adage about a glass of water: It's either half full or half empty. The truth is, however, that if we see that same glass of water as we view our comfort zone, we could observe that life is incomplete in one direction or depleting in the other. We must choose to see it not in a state of being but, instead, in a state of motion. What if we poured water *into* the glass? Our glass then becomes fuller. Life becomes fuller!

What makes life so magical is our perspective. Perspective shapes how you see and feel *everything*, which in turn shapes what you do and ultimately what happens next.

Everything comes down to choices. And you do indeed have a say in the matter. The effects of disruption are a choice. Innovation is a choice.

The world needs ideas. The world needs *your* ideas.

Ralph Waldo Emerson once observed that the only person you are destined to become is the person you decide to be.

Transformation and disruption will happen. But it's all a matter of perspective. Change will either happen to you or because of you. The same is true for innovation.

Who do you decide to be? Again, it *is* your choice.

With opportunity comes possibility. What the world needs right now is for you to become the greatest version of you.

Innovation isn't just for the likes of Nikola Tesla, Steve Jobs, Patricia Bath, and Katherine Johnson.

Everyone has the ability to be innovative. We all hope, aspire, have ideas, imagine, dream, give in to curiosity, create and are creative in our own ways, and want what's best for those we care about. Collectively, these are the pillars of innovation.

Innovation is a superpower. It's *your* superpower. You have the ability to unlock it not only within yourself but in those around you as well.

Somewhere inside of you right now is a place where nothing is impossible. Somewhere inside of the person next to you is an idea that can change the course of history.

To make the world a better place, share your ideas. To make the world a better place together, unshackle the ideas trapped in those around you. This is how you change the future. You visualize the art of the possible and work with one another to bring to life what didn't exist or couldn't prevail otherwise.

Meaningful change, the kind of change that makes a dent in the universe, is made by people who are not reticent to dream out loud, who are not afraid to be different, who are not too complacent to be great together.

Innovation, like leadership, is about empowering yourself *and* empowering others.

Do what's necessary. Explore what's possible. Then do what was previously impossible. This is your destiny. It's what you do with it that defines your legacy.

Carla has charted the path forward for you. I can't wait to see what you do.

—**Brian Solis**, digital anthropologist, futurist,
optimist, and author of *Lifescale*

Introduction

I t was the end of teaching a summer course in Colorado Springs, and Katharine couldn't wait for one last adventure before she returned to Massachusetts. The group headed out to Pike's Peak, one of Colorado's 58 fourteeners—a mountain that tops out at over 14,000 feet. After a ride to the summit, she took a long, deep breath and savored the 360-degree view.

As a college professor, scholar, former journalist, and social activist, Katharine was also a prolific writer. She cared deeply about urban poverty, social injustice, and sexism—and how to right them. As she stood atop the mountain, the memories of what she'd observed on her travels across the country came flooding back, sights such as the white buildings in Chicago and the wheat fields of Kansas. She was struck by the expansive views of the plains spreading out into the distance and the emotions the experience evoked in her.

When she got back to her hotel room, she began scribbling out the lines to a poem, which she finished before she left Colorado Springs. She'd set it aside for a few years before submitting it to a publisher to commemorate the Fourth of July. Once it was distributed to the broader public, Katharine was taken aback at how fast people picked it up and its overwhelming popularity. Eventually put to music, this poem took observations of the good and bad within a country, distilled it into a people's optimism about the future, and related that into her own work as a writer. The result is one of the most extraordinary songs in US history: "America the Beautiful."

At the top of Pike's Peak in 1893, Katharine Lee Bates didn't set out to write words that described the idealism of a country. She didn't intend to pen a song that rivaled "The Star-Spangled Banner" as a national anthem. She simply connected the dots between what she'd observed in her travels, distilled them into a pattern, related that into her work, and out came the idea for her poem—one she no doubt edited many times to get it just right before she pitched it to a magazine for publication, and one that's had an extraordinary impact on generations of people.

Katharine never held an official innovation title in any of her jobs, yet she was one of the most prolific innovators in history. Her work consistently delivered extraordinary outcomes. As a professor at Wellesley College, she mentored young poets such as Robert Frost. She helped establish American literature as a field of study in college. Katharine traveled internationally and earned a master of arts degree during a time when women barely left the comfort of their parlors. As a journalist, she sought to change stereotypes of down-trodden people. As a social activist, she considered herself a global citizen who worked fervently for world peace.

Katharine is only one example of why we need to rethink how we define innovation, who's involved, and how it's done.

Because we're leaving a significant number of opportunities on the table that can make an extraordinary impact on the world in which we live.

My Inspiration for This Book

In old-fashioned paper memos, there was a line that read "RE:" for "regarding." It let people know the topic of the memo they were about to read. With that as my inspiration, the title of this book comes from regarding the way we think about innovation = RE:Think Innovation.

I want to change the way we think about innovation.

Since I was in second grade, people have told me it wasn't my place to raise my hand with a new idea. It was someone else's responsibility: Someone older, someone with a degree, someone with a different degree, someone with more degrees, someone more serious, someone more conceptual, someone with a specific job title, someone with accreditation letters behind their name, someone with…you can fill in the blank with a slew of random credentials.

The message was clear: Innovators were a special breed. I wasn't one of them.

Except I was. I knew it in my heart, I just didn't know how to prove it

It's taken nearly five years for me to write this book. The one question I sought to answer was this: Is coming up with a great idea that has a big impact a process people can learn? I conducted interviews and research into hundreds of innovators in all walks of life. I started out asking about how they came up with their big ideas. Most couldn't tell me. So instead, I asked questions that walked them backwards through time to understand the path of their idea starting with its inspiration. Once we had reverse engineered it, the person then recognized that they followed the same process over and over. It was an eye-opening revelation to them and further confirmation for me of a tried-and-true process. Not only was the framework much simpler than they realized, it also helped tell a story of a new idea in a way that made it feel more familiar and less risky.

Then, I took the process and put it to the test in the real world. I actively sought out left-brain analytical thinkers and conceptual right-brain visionaries. I worked it through with C-suite executives, traditional innovation groups, frontline employees, volunteers, and everyday people who would *never* label themselves as innovators. Around the world I shared and taught it in speeches, workshops, consulting, and one-on-one coaching.

It worked. Every time.

I wrote this book for three reasons:

1. To teach people a simple, scalable process that anyone, at any level, with any experience, can learn and use to consistently come up with great ideas. In fact, it's my goal to personally teach one million people how to become innovators by 2025.

2. To make it clear that there's no single "type" of person who makes the best innovator. Everyone has their natural genius. But, if we're going to succeed as teams, much less entire organizations, we have to empower people to use their own way of innovating and appreciate what each style contributes. You'll begin to recognize and even create opportunities that your competitors miss once you harness the collective powers of your larger organization. It builds a culture of respect and trust, and ultimately, extraordinary outcomes.

3. To de-bunk the myth that innovation has to be complex, time-consuming, and expensive. There's plenty of disruption that follows new ideas, but not all innovation requires that level of upside-down thinking. For many of the companies I studied, it was the cumulative effect of giving unconventional thinkers opportunities to contribute that made the difference. This also helped remove the elitist stereotype that came with innovation. One of the reasons I use people's first names in the pages that follow is to take the formality out of the stories. Mr., Ms., and last names create hierarchy and emotional distance. Being on a first-name basis with someone means you know each other well. I want you to feel you know the people and stories in this book as well as I do.

This Book Is for You If...

...you're an executive who's frustrated with the complexity, cost, and culture of your innovation focus. If you feel that you're constantly pushing that huge boulder uphill trying to reach your (or your company's) full potential but never get higher than false summits. And, if you're exhausted with the effort and dealing with the psychological impact of constantly dashed hopes and feelings of failure.

...you're a team lead who believes your crew is capable of much more but can't figure out how to draw it out of them. Who wants to build a brand and a track record as a successful innovator but doesn't know what to do, doesn't think you have time, or tries through rigid processes rather than by bringing out the best in people.

...you believe in innovation with a little "i" as much as a big, disruptive one. Who's had to deal with the brunt of massive change and upheaval that cascades down from the top under the dictate to drive synergies, leverage strengths, and think outside the box.

...you've ever heard that little voice inside tell you that you have a great idea. The one that pops into your head and screams for your attention before reason convinces you it's ridiculous, and you'll look stupid if you say it out loud. And day after day, another little piece dies inside of you because you've squelched that urge to do extraordinary things for so long that you no longer believe that you can.

My wish for you is to feel competent, confident, and empowered to do work that has purpose, makes you proud of how you spend your days, and has a bigger impact on your world than you ever dreamed possible.

Now, go be extraordinary.

CHAPTER 1

What Is Innovation?

I t was a hot, humid day in Orlando as Marc Duke caught up with his business partner. It was 1990, and they'd gotten together because his colleague had an ingenious idea he wanted to run past Marc.

While walking down an aisle in the grocery store, Marc's associate noticed something: On one side he saw row after row of soft drinks. On the other, pet food. What if you could take the refreshing essence of a soft drink and package it up for the pet market? Marc, a 47-year-old former ad man and basset hound owner, believed they were onto something.

That's when the partners launched their new venture: the Original Pet Drink Company. The duo believed that regular tap water—laden with chlorine, lead, and bacteria—wasn't good for the four-legged loves of their lives. Hoping to tap into the $17 billion (and growing) that pet lovers spent on their beloved darlings, they entered the market with their Thirsty Dog! and Thirsty Cat! specialty water.

These carbonated, vitamin-enriched beverages retailed for $1.79 and came in two flavors. Crispy Beef for dogs had beef bouillon with a hint of sweetness. Tangy Fish was a bit like salmon in a butter sauce. The Food and Drug Administration approved the water as fit for human consumption, and it was even kosher.

Ad Age quoted Marc as asking, "Once you give people more than water to drink, they do. Why shouldn't pets have that option, too?" He predicted the pet soda market would reach $500 million by 2004.

Within two months, Marc's company was shipping 175,000 bottles of beef- and salmon-flavored premium pet water every week to stores around the United States. The testing the company had done during research and development plus the 100 formula tweaks they'd made seemed to be paying off.

At least for a while.

The goal of the specialty water was to give pets healthy skin and thicker, healthier fur. However, vets questioned the need for the specialty drink. At 200 calories a bottle, the sugar-laden refresher made a pet's tendency toward obesity even worse. On top of that, once customers tallied up the long-term cost of Thirsty Dog! and Thirsty Cat! water compared to the free-from-the-tap version, the sheen wore off. In the long run, buyers believed their pets probably didn't care what they drank—considering their four-legged friends gave themselves whole-body tongue baths and quenched their thirst from the toilet.

Experts now consider the Thirsty Dog! and Thirsty Cat! line of waters one of the biggest product flops in history. I'd venture that the execs of the Original Pet Drink Company probably thought they were incredibly innovative with the launch of their new idea.

But the deeper question is, did they really understand innovation to begin with?

What Are We Searching For?

If you asked 10 different people to define innovation, you'd get 20 different responses.

It's one of those things that seems simple to define and understand but turns complicated when you're pressed for specifics. It's no wonder. *Innovation* has turned into one of the biggest cliché words executives use to talk about how they differentiate their companies and lead industries but never actually define or explain. The truth is, we don't have a common, agreed-upon definition of innovation. That's because people have a hard time understanding and recognizing it, much less defining it.

Let's take a look at some of the definitions from industry experts:

We define innovation as creativity plus delivery, helping our clients transform their innovation performance by focusing on four requirements for innovating at scale: strategy, pipeline of ideas, execution, and organization. (McKinsey & Company)

Innovation is the process through which value is created and delivered to a community of users in the form of a new solution. (*Fast Company*)

...an approach...that addresses a major imminent want or need that people have, [something] they know they want or need or that they will want or need once we provide it. (George Damis Yancopoulos, president of Regeneron Laboratories and chief scientific officer of Regeneron Pharmaceutical)

Innovation generally refers to changing processes or creating more effective processes, products and ideas. (Department of Industry, Australian government)

An innovation is a feasible relevant offering such as a product, service, process or experience with a viable business model that is perceived as new and is adopted by customers. (Gijs van Wulfen, author of the FORTH innovation methodology)

Can you actually tell me what innovation is after reading those definitions? I can't, and I make a living in this line of work!

Innovation is an amazing thing that can have a tremendous number of benefits, but does anyone really know what it is? I'm guessing that even if you had *your* company's definition in front of you, you'd still feel confused.

> People have a hard time defining innovation because they don't understand it themselves.

This is because people have a hard time explaining something they don't understand themselves.

For example, most people confuse innovation and creativity. They think they are synonymous, but that's because they misunderstand the relationship between them. It's especially important for business leaders who compete in an innovation-driven world to get the difference, because it's a huge deal when it comes to a company's culture.

Creativity

Most of us think of creativity as a unique talent that relates to art—the ability to paint, sculpt, draw, compose music, or do anything that's expressive. More broadly defined, creativity is the mental ability to imagine new, unusual, or unique ideas.

The *Creativity Research Journal* points out that originality is vital for creativity, but it's not enough. For me, creativity is bringing a new perspective to anything and having it add value. Investing in creativity is almost a loss leader—it won't make money as soon as you invest in it. But six months down the road, you'll begin to see a change in the performance of both employees and your overall company for having encouraged it.

Innovation

Not only is this a confusing word, but it's also intimidating because of how it's thrown around in business today—especially disruptive innovation.

The distinction between creativity and innovation is important because one can't exist without the other in any environment. It's impossible to develop a truly innovative company if creativity isn't recognized, appreciated, and nurtured. And without effective processes to transform creative thinking into practical, high-value applications, creativity doesn't mean squat.

Yet, when people think of both of these topics, they think of creativity as optional and innovation as a business necessity.

To be fair, there's a lot of pressure on the C-suite to focus on innovation. As the world adopts new, fast, and frequently changing technologies, businesses scramble to keep up through digital transformation and changing customer expectations. Execs want to prevent customer churn and revenue slumps. Boards of directors demand agility and efficiency, and they have keen memories of the Kodaks, Borderses, and Polaroids of the world who failed to keep pace with change. They look at the likes of Amazon and Netflix and see that innovation is where the money is. The fact that it's not happening either quickly or consistently means that it has to be hard to understand, right? There's no CEO or executive consultant who would last a day if they didn't tell the story of how they, personally, understand the complexity, complicated processes, high-dollar investments, and bloated teams that make it a reality.

Innovation isn't actually complex at all—once you stop trying to make it that way. Here's the definition of *innovation* that I've developed over more than 20 years of doing this work.

**Innovation is about consistently coming up
with new, great, and reliable ideas.**

It doesn't matter where in the organization you work, what your title is, or how long you've been there. An innovation culture understands why you need all three of these attributes to be successful. When you only have one, your approach to innovation isn't sustainable.

Let's take a look at the characteristics of new, great, and reliable ideas.

New Ideas

Look at the news from any business media outlet and you'll see that every company is being told to innovate. Experts tout executing on new ideas as the savior for bigger market share, bigger customers, and bigger revenues. That's music to every shareholder's ears.

However, when companies hunt for new ideas for the sake of new ideas, their efforts invariably fall flat. Coca-Cola tried New Coke before rebranding it Coke II and going back to the original recipe. Myspace tried moving into entertainment and music after users jumped ship for Facebook. Colgate launched a line of frozen foods (Colgate beef lasagna anyone?). Bic tried extending its brand into disposable underwear and pantyhose. Frito-Lay made a Cheetos lip balm. Swedish weapons manufacturer Bofors added toothpaste to its product line. Harley-Davidson tried its hand at cologne. R.J. Reynolds found its smokeless cigarettes a tough sell, especially when the company's own CEO said, "It tastes like shit and smells like a fart. We spent $350 million and ended up with a turd with a tip."

People think coming up with new things is the answer to business growth without understanding why or even if they should create new things in the first place. We think new = good simply because it's new. A lot of innovation is actually just coming up with a new idea, assuming it's good because it's new, and then watching it crash and burn.

A new idea can be something completely disruptive, like personal computers, video streaming, or smartphones. But to be a new idea, it doesn't have to be completely revolutionary. It can simply take the essence behind another successful idea and massage it to fit in a new, yet drastically different, environment. For example, the BMW iDrive system was inspired by the video controls from the gaming industry. Retired aeronautical engineer Owen Maclaren used the idea of an airplane's retractable landing gear to develop the first lightweight foldable baby stroller. McDonald's based its drive-through design on the principles of a fast Formula 1 pit stop. A new idea simply needs to go beyond the same old thing that's always been done and bring in fresh inspiration from the outside world. At its root, a new idea is something that's unexpected.

But truly innovative companies understand that being new is just one aspect of a successful idea.

Great Ideas

A great idea makes you feel really good. It inspires you, gets you excited, and engages you emotionally. It has a big *wow!* factor. David Ogilvy describes great ideas as the ones that make you gasp when you first see them and make you jealous you didn't think of them yourself. Whether people realize they needed the idea or not, it creates appeal and excitement.

I'll be honest, *great* is much more of a subjective term than either *new* or *reliable*.

A great idea is something that people actually want. The business landscape is awash with ideas that seemed revolutionary but ended up failing because there was no value to be delivered (or the value didn't match the price tag), and therefore there wasn't a market demand.

We were once big fans of brands that are long gone. AOL was an early pioneer in the mid-1990s of using the internet to connect people. As the first company to open up access to the internet en masse, AOL was the most recognized brand on the web in the United States. The PalmPilot helped people organize their lives. It was the first true personal digital assistant and sported a touch screen, stylus, and apps that helped you manage your calendar and tasks and synced with your desktop computer. Of the original handful of social media sites, Myspace had the greatest popularity and influence. MapQuest was the first commercial mapping service that let people pitch their oversized atlas. TiVo gave people freedom from their TV with the ability to pause, rewind, and record TV. All were incredibly innovative in their prime. But when's the last time you talked about any of them other than as the butt of a joke?

Coming up with an idea that's a great idea is the first step. However, if the only redeeming quality of your idea is that it's great, your innovation strategy won't last. You've seen companies like these come out of the box and experience amazing, huge success.

Everybody went crazy over them…but they had one great idea. That's the best they ever did, and their shooting star quickly fizzled.

It's not enough for an idea just to be great. You have to be able to rely on it for the long run.

Reliable Ideas

A reliable idea is one on which you can build your business. It will make your company money. It doesn't matter how cool or exciting your idea may sound, if it's out of scope for your business, it's not the direction you should go, or if doesn't tie into the purpose of your company, then it's not feasible.

You can execute a reliable idea. It contributes to the growth of your organization and has a cost benefit. This could be in generating revenue, saving money, using resources (people, time, equipment, etc.) more efficiently, or any other way of delivering financial value.

Reliable ideas also have longevity. There's the telephone in all of its iterations. Portable music players and being able to carry a thousand songs in your pocket, as Apple showed us, or the ability to Shazam a tune. Think of how the travel industry changed when people could book airline and hotel reservations directly. All of these ideas have endured the test of time.

There are a lot of ideas we wouldn't rely on (flashing back to Colgate's frozen lasagna meals). To be considered innovative, you must deliver ideas that people can trust will turn into something that delivers the results you want.

But reliability in and of itself isn't enough to make your company innovative. There are business that have one highly reliable idea, and then over time they just cling to that success. After their initial boom, they never really come out with anything new. Every other idea turns into just a slightly different twist on their first success. Companies like Blockbuster and Sears were guilty of this. They both had ideas that served them well for decades, but ultimately that wasn't enough to withstand changes in either of their industries. The glory days were too great to let go of, so they never did. And we know how those strategies worked out.

People say coming up with ideas is the easy part. It's the execution that makes or breaks innovation. I beg to differ. I believe that the reason most ideas are so hard to implement is because they don't have all three aspects of success: being new, great, and reliable.

A new idea surprises and delights people because it's unexpected.

A great idea inspires and excites you.

A reliable idea makes you money.

Our task is to consistently come up with new, great, and reliable ideas.

The Perpetual Innovators

When all three of these criteria come together in ideas on a consistent basis, you have what it takes to build an iconic, innovative company. I call these brands and the people behind them Perpetual Innovators.

Perpetual Innovators have a consistent track record of new, great, and reliable ideas. Organizations that are persistent and open to new things welcome experimentation. They understand that every new idea has a height that plays out, and that's when they identify the next opportunity. They're able to deliver innovative ideas consistently over a long period of time—decades or even centuries. They get people—both employees and the outside world—excited about what they do, because others want to see what comes around the next corner. These are the Amazons, the Googles, and the Teslas of every industry. They've made perpetual innovation something that's an innate part of their culture.

Look at Netflix, one of the most successful Perpetual Innovators in the history of business. It started as a front-door DVD delivery service that rivaled movie-rental stores like Blockbuster. As a Perpetual Innovator, the company has grown through subscriptions to a physical product to subscriptions to a streaming one. It wooed a team of writers and developers so it could deliver original content. The brand created prestige and credibility for itself through shows like *House of Cards* and *Orange Is the New Black.* Netflix continually innovates the experience with new, great, and reliable ideas that remove pain points before subscribers realize they exist.

Don't want to click to watch the next episode? No problem—Netflix now has a six-second countdown that takes away the need to decide. Too impatient to sit through the trailer on each episode of your favorite show? No problem—just click to skip the intro. Through consistent, perpetual innovation, Netflix has revolutionized the way people watch movies and TV shows.

Innovative companies like Netflix—the Perpetual Innovators—do this because the leaders of the organization and the employees who work there have a clear definition and understanding of innovation.

You, the Innovator

Consistently delivering new, great, and reliable ideas comes from practicing it so much that it that turns the process into a habit. Creativity and critical thinking are like any other muscle—if you want to strengthen it, you have to use it. You have to push it beyond its normal boundaries and apply pressure from different directions. You must practice making it perform under different situations, time frames, and terrains. The more consistently you do anything, the better you get.

> Perpetual Innovators are the elite athletes of ideas. They consistently hone their skills so they can draw on them without giving it a thought. The pressure of a situation or deadline doesn't deter them.

Perpetual Innovators are the elite athletes of ideas. They consistently hone their skills so they can draw on them without giving it a thought. The pressure of a situation or deadline doesn't deter them, because their ability to jump in at a moment's notice is deeply practiced. While we like to think that these people are creative geniuses, it turns out that the only difference is that the "geniuses" have more practice than other people.

The ability to build a practice that draws on all three characteristics of an idea creates an organizational culture conditioned to deliver extraordinary outcomes. If you don't have all three, you will struggle to produce the opportunities your employees deserve to bring forward, your company deserves to deliver, and your stakeholders deserve to enjoy.

While there's a lot of focus on companies and their ability to innovate, here's what I want *you* to know.

You have the ability to become one of the most iconic Perpetual Innovators the world has ever seen. Whether it's you as an individual, you as a leader in your organization, or your company in the market you serve. Maybe you're a small business owner, an entrepreneur, or the CEO of a Fortune 50 company. It doesn't matter.

Regardless of who you are or where you work, *you can become a Perpetual Innovator.*

Let's take a look at why you aren't one already.

CHAPTER 2

Why Don't We Innovate?

I could hear the stress in his voice in just the first few minutes of our call.

Mohamed worked for a start-up research and development company based in Canada. He was in the thick of planning the launch of the company's new software, but he was stuck. He and the executive team wanted to build a strong emotional connection with their customers and simplify how they talked about the software. But the sophistication of their platform and their push for disrupting an industry made their story convoluted. That's why they wanted my help. Mohamed and his executive team needed a marketing strategy as innovative as the product itself.

One day as we were thrashing through a strategy, I asked Mohamed what brand inspired him.

"Disney," he said. "Because it doesn't matter where you enter the brand—theme parks, movies, or a retail store—you always have an amazing experience."

Disney then became our measuring stick. "If Disney built a learning management platform," we asked ourselves, "what decisions would they make?"

The first goal Mohamed had was to become the go-to resource for how teachers, administrators, parents, and students looked at learning. Just like Disney has its Disney Institute blog that teaches people and companies about how to deliver stellar customer experiences, he wanted to set the standard for how people looked at education and then set their expectations. We laid it all out in a strategy document, which Mohamed then took to the executive team for approval.

That's when the wheels fell off the bus.

As Mohamed wrapped up his presentation, the chief financial officer put his pencil down. He pushed himself back from the table, crossed his fleshy arms across his broad chest, pursed his lips, and said, "We're not doing this. We're nothing like Disney. We don't have dogs. We don't have princesses. And we don't have theme parks. We are a serious company with PhDs. We have engineers. We're smart professionals who take the work we do seriously. What you've proposed is ridiculous. If we're going to show people how innovative we are, I need you to go back to your desk and come up with some ads that tell people we're innovative. I need you to update the website. And I need you to start doing cold calls. This is how we get people to know that we're innovative—by *telling* them we are."

That's when Mohamed's shoulders drooped. He hung his head. And he went back to his desk. Instead of coming to work every day with a spring in his step, excited to become the "Disney" of learning management software, he did the same boring work that other people in his industry were stuck doing—ads, cold calls, and web pages that were actually sales brochures.

Although this nimble, starry-eyed start-up touted innovation, Mohamed's idea of what that looked like was distinctly different from that of his executive team.

Has this ever happened to you?

Walk the Talk

Nearly every organization in existence today touts its innovation chops. They list it as a value, insist it's their market differentiator, and claim to invest in it wholeheartedly.

But if you look under the hood of a majority of these businesses, they fail miserably at walking the talk. While they may have a definition of innovation that they understand, moving from that point into execution is a gap they haven't been able to navigate. Either the general employee population doesn't understand how to move forward with an innovation directive, or, like Mohamed's leadership team, they don't believe that they're the type of company to innovate like others.

During my research, I've found that there are three big, common reasons why people and companies don't step forth and make progress with innovation:

- They overcomplicate it.
- They think it's only something others know how to do.
- They don't how to do it.

Overcomplication

Innovation isn't impossible. But it usually doesn't work because we see it as a complex process that we have to work hard to grasp. Why? Because we've been taught that the more complex something is, the more credible it is and the more likely it is to work. There's actually a term for this: complexity bias, the belief that complex solutions and ideas are always better than simple ones. When we have to choose between two options, we often ignore the simpler, faster, cheaper, or easier one because we think it's *too* simple. Nothing that easy could actually work! So, to us, innovation can't be a simple or straightforward process, because if it were, it wouldn't *be* innovation.

Contrary to the complexity bias, the simplest answers usually are the best ones. It goes back to Occam's razor: the simplest solution is most likely the right one.

Let me give you an example. A couple of years ago I suffered from deep fatigue. It didn't matter what I did; I just couldn't shake it. I'm not a coffee drinker, so I explained to my doctor that it couldn't be caffeine. Iron deficiency? The bloodwork came back clean. I exercised. Cut back on sugar and processed foods. Counted carbs and made sure I got enough legit sunlight. Nothing worked.

Then my doctor asked an all-revealing (and embarrassingly simple) question: How much sleep do you get?

It couldn't be something that easy, could it?

But it was. As a parent with young kids, a business owner, and frequent traveler, I realized I was squeezing by on four to five hours a night, instead of the eight or even nine I really needed. My complexity bias, however, made this simple answer hard to accept. However, once I started hitting the hay earlier and for more hours, my fatigue vanished.

So why do we have this complexity bias? And why can't we accept the idea that innovation might actually be simple? Our fascination for complexity leads to bigger, more emotionally driven problem. If a problem is simple, then you should know how to solve it. And when you don't, it makes you feel... well...dumb. Therefore, by adding layer upon layer of complexity to a situation, you're able to rationalize your way out of understanding it.

Let's pretend your career's clicking along and you're enjoying your vice president status and corner office. The day comes when you hire a herd of McKinsey consultants to help with an innovation challenge. Team McKinsey comes in, takes a look around and points out how simple the solution is. So simple, in fact, they can't believe you missed it. As the responsible party who brought them in, that would probably cost you your job. Companies—and the executives who run them—put a whole lotta weight in complexity, not simplicity. It's what makes you feel important, and like you have credibility and value.

For many, innovation is about "big bangs" and multimillion-dollar investments—the kinds that disrupt industries and turn markets upside down. These set unrealistic expectations that bring white-knuckled risk with them because the cost of failure can end careers and put organizations out of business. They drive people's emotions around their job and work responsibilities. You want to feel important, not incompetent or out of your league. But complexity and simplicity are opposite extremes, and leaders have to understand that not all innovation demands a complicated process.

> Complexity and simplicity are opposite extremes, and leaders have to understand that not all innovation demands a complicated process.

Leaders will need a leap of faith that one of the greatest problems with innovation is the perception that it's too complicated. It actually can be very simple, and there's nothing wrong with that. Yes, you look at iconic brands like Apple, Google, Tesla, or any number of others and say, "I could never be that innovative." But perhaps you're selling yourself short too quickly.

It's Something Others Do

In the world of great ideas, iconic brands get all the credit.

Take LEGO, for example. This is a company that sells little rectangular pieces of plastic. But they consistently churn out great idea after great idea. Go to their website and, besides ordering products, you can build things, share them with friends, and watch videos. Five times a year they publish a magazine that kids go crazy over. They produced *Beyond the Brick: A LEGO Brickumentary*—a documentary for adult fans of LEGO bricks. They released Hollywood feature films that grossed hundreds of millions of dollars. Their YouTube channel has millions of subscribers. There's even have a game you can download from the app store.

Toms Shoes gives away a pair of shoes for everyone you buy. Domino's Pizza is now called a tech company. Red Bull is a media empire that happens to sell energy drinks.

And even business-to-business (B2B) brands like IBM are hard to top. Their team of engineers built the smartest machine in the world and then took it on national TV to compete again world's smartest minds. GE's Ecomagination was a groundbreaking strategy the company used to build more efficient machines that produce cleaner energy, reduce greenhouse gas emissions, clean water and cut its use, and make money while doing it. And Volvo's B2B division hired one of the world's most famous stuntmen to do a split between two semitrucks.

Now, brands like all of these create a big problem for you and me.

If I'm a household cleaning company, I'm not going to create the world's smartest machine and compete on national TV with it. If I work in pharmaceuticals, I'm not going to give shoes away for free. And if I'm in environmental cleanup, there's no way that I'm going to spend the money to launch a Hollywood feature film.

A number of years ago I was at a conference listening to a speaker from Zappos talk about their approach to customer experience. Since I work primarily with B2B brands and was consulting for a boron mining company at the time, none of what the Zappos speaker talked about felt relatable to me. As I sat in the audience, my mind began to wander. I scrolled through my social media feed to see what was going on in the "real" world and looked around the room for someone I could catch up with over cocktails.

A few weeks after that, I thought about this particular scenario. Out of curiosity, I did an internet search on my behavior. It turns out that what happened to me is actually a psychological phenomenon called Brand Detachment Disorder.

**Brand Detachment Disorder is the tendency we have to
dismiss the relevancy of great ideas because we think
that what we do is different or unique.**

And it turns out that you suffer from BDD just as much as I do. When someone talks about Virgin Airlines and how great they are, I hear people say they don't have that kind of budget. Or bring up Microsoft, Marvel Studios, or Salesforce, and you'll hear a slew of excuses:

We don't have that kind of budget.
Our team is too big and can't be that agile.
We have too much bureaucracy.
We need more processes.
Our company is more serious.
Our company isn't that serious
My boss is a control freak.
My boss is emotionally MIA.
Our sales cycle is too long.
Our sales cycle is too short.
What we sell is too boring.
It's too consumer oriented, and we're a B2B company.
That's more business focused, and our target is consumers.

Everyone makes excuses for why they can't be more creative. After I gave a speech in Stockholm, Sweden, a man from Red Bull came up to talk to me. He said BDD hit home for him. When I asked what brand he envies, he said Coca-Cola. "If I just had Coke's budget...the things I could do!" If someone from Red Bull—a company that sets the bar high for every other company out there—is making excuses for why they can't be more creative, this is a syndrome that afflicts *everyone*.

We have to stop discounting great work from inspiring brands and instead use them for our own inspiration, because these are the kinds of brands that set the expectations for every one of our customers. Ignoring them sets the stage for our own mediocrity and gives every employee an excuse to stick with the status quo.

The recovery for Brand Detachment Disorder begins when we admit that we have a problem. But we have to catch ourselves in the moment when we're exhibiting BDD and nip it in the bud right then and there.

Think about this: You're back at the office and someone from sales says to you, "We need to do a cool video like Land Rover did when it drove up the 999 stairs to Heaven's Gate in China!" and you roll your eyes. That's a sign you have Brand Detachment Disorder. When someone from human resources says, "We need to create something that will go viral like the ALS ice bucket challenge!" and you cross your arms and grimace, that's a clear sign you're in the midst of Brand Detachment Disorder. Or, if your boss says (again), "We need a team that's going to become 'the ultimate driving machine' for our industry, just like BMW," and you want to reach across the desk and strangle her...that's a *clear* sign you're suffering from Brand Detachment Disorder!

If you catch yourself feeling certain that your tiny budget and small staff could never manage to embrace the mindset of publicly traded companies with billion-dollar valuations, think again. Because once you've raised your awareness, you'll be able to recognize BDD in your everyday behavior. If you don't, you'll end up with the business-as-usual stale ideas and status-quo thinking. When you tune out creativity from wherever it comes, you lose the opportunity for inspiration.

We Don't Know How

Maybe you're ready, willing, and perfectly able to dive into innovation, but you just don't know where to start. This can be one of the most frustrating situations in which to find yourself. There's a tremendous amount of information on the market about how to innovate, but it feels like you need a PhD, a hefty budget, and a team of consultants to hold your hand.

Trust me, it doesn't have to be that way.

It's a common misconception that to become innovative, you just need to generate ideas. Successful innovation, however, involves homework before you get into a room with your colleagues and start sharing whatever comes to mind. And there's plenty of vetting that has to happen after the fact to ensure that the ideas you come up with are actually executable.

Innovation is easier than we think because there actually is a consistent process you can learn (and teach) to show you the way. If you're looking for hope to get things rolling, this is exactly what you've been waiting for.

In the next chapter, you'll learn the five-step process that the most prolific innovators in the world use. It's so simple that anyone at any level, in any organization, and in any industry can use it to get better at innovation. By following this process over and over again, you'll become a Perpetual Innovator who will consistently deliver remarkable ideas that turn into extraordinary outcomes for your business.

How to Use the Rest of This Book

I hear too many people say they don't have good ideas, or they don't know how to come up with them. It's important that everyone in your organization— no matter how big or small, how old or new, or what kind of industry you're in—learns to connect the dots between life around them and the work they do. This book is for engineers and artists, marketers and accountants, PTA presidents and nonprofit volunteers. Learning a process to come up with, vet, and share ideas can be used to solve all kinds of problems whether you're at work or home. You'll find the idea-generation process you learn in this book helpful to not only climb the corporate ladder, but also make life more exciting, connected, and fun. There're infinite possibilities that come with new ideas.

This book is for those of you who believe that our best, most creative, and most innovative days of business are ahead. That innovative thinking is a skill that's both taught and learned. And that this is the key to the future of a business's ability to create opportunities and thrive.

Now, let's get down to business.

PART 1
How to Innovate

The Perpetual Innovation Process

In 1999, Carey Smith started a company called the HVLS Fan Co. This name (an acronym for *High Volume Low Speed*) described the types of fans his company sold: massively big ones that move a huge amount of air but at very low speeds. They're the kinds you see hanging from ceilings in places that aren't practical to air-condition, such as gyms, dairy barns, fairground buildings, churches, event centers, bars, and airports.

In the early days, it was Carey and a handful of people sitting around the table getting the business off the ground. "We had one phone," he said. "When it rang, whoever was closest answered it, saying, 'High Volume Low Speed Fan Company, can I help you?' Inevitably, there was a long pause on the other end until the person finally asked, 'Are you the people who sell those big-ass fans?'"

Carey admitted he's no marketing genius, but he knew a good idea when he heard one. It didn't take him long to change the name of the company to Big Ass Fans.

"What the name tells you is that the company is very contrarian. We don't look at things the way others do. We don't think about products or marketing the way other people do. The name appealed to us because we thought it would be like wearing a ponytail. Where we could basically say in a manner of speaking that we don't care what you think; we do things the way we do things." Carey also showed he didn't care what other people thought when he donned the title chief big ass.

This mindset was a big part of the culture as he grew his company. It's something he had experienced firsthand years earlier at a deli in Ann Arbor, Michigan.

Driving down the street looking for a place to grab lunch, Carey saw a line out the front door of Zingerman's Deli. He knew that was a good sign for his growling stomach.

He parked, got in line, and slowly inched his way inside. Once there, he looked around. This was not your typical deli. There were entire display cases of meats, cheeses, and other exotic items that weren't your run-of-the-mill, quickie-mart-type sandwich makings.

"They bought the best cheeses, meats, and condiments, and they baked their bread fresh every day," explained Carey. "You weren't going to get crap ingredients, because they built the best sandwich in the world. And that's how they approached their entire business."

When he ordered his sandwich, it wasn't an apathetic high-school kid slinging a basket across the counter. "They were hippy-dippy types and different to talk to. They liked to kid around and joke, but they delivered a great product. The employees knew why an Amish chicken breast or Arkansas peppered ham had their own unique flavors and textures. They could tell you what part of Switzerland Emmental cheese was from and how the taste compared to handmade fresh mozzarella. Everyone there was smart and made business fun. That motivated me," Carey said.

There was a lot about Zingerman's Deli that he transplanted into Big Ass Fans—especially the idea of going against popular opinion about making money and instead, focusing on quality.

"Just like I saw that day at Zingerman's, Big Ass Fans does the whole thing differently. The name on the outside is indicative of what's going on inside. You're driven by it, or you aren't. The name expresses who we are and why we do what we do. It'd be hard for the people who work here to make a standard ceiling fan or light bulb."

Carey understood that having a brand that says it values a quality product is one thing. But consistently coming up with new, great, and reliable ideas that turn it into a reality is another. Big Ass Fans' headquarters was in Lexington, Kentucky, but its biggest competitors were companies that made low-end fans in China by the millions fast and cheap. They didn't use real wood or metal, and they used the cheapest motors they could find. Then, they made up revenue in maintenance, repairs, or replacement fans.

He realized that if he could make quality his secret sauce, that would inspire customers to keep coming back. And that's exactly what happened.

"What's interesting about Zingerman's is that it has grown larger over the years, but it's not a Kroger. It's not a Whole Foods," Carey said. "They recognized that there's a limit to what they can do. They won't sell salami to everyone in the country. To be the best, they have to focus on a smaller market, and they can't be everything to everybody. We're in the same boat…We're not a high-volume manufacturer, either. We started out making a couple of hundred fans a year. If you make a decision that you're going to focus on quality, you limit your volume."

As Carey and his team focused more and more on quality, that brought them closer to their customers. They looked for constant feedback to help them deliver new, great, and reliable products every single day. Big Ass Fans' customers came to trust the "ingredients" and the employees of the company.

Carey's small-time start-up grew into a successful business that's won a slew of awards for innovation and been named one of Fortune's 50 Best Workplaces for Recent College Graduates. It's also one that he sold to a private equity firm in 2017 for $500 million.

Why was Carey so successful? He understands some key things that have made him a Perpetual Innovator.

"Most people assume they lack creativity," he pointed out. "That's not the case. It's that they're afraid of failure. You have bright kids who have a 4.0 in high school or college, and they'll fail because they're not willing to take a risk.

"People are conformists. I've been in customer situations where people are conservative in terms of business, and they're afraid to do anything different. Other companies would like to work with us, but it might disturb their channels. Public companies are even worse because CEOs don't want to give up control of anything.

"It's safe, but it has to be an awfully boring place to be."

The Perpetual Innovation Process™

As we look at innovation and what consistently leads to new, great, and reliable ideas, it's time to dig into the process that the most innovative people and teams in the world use—people like Carey and his teams at Big Ass Fans. As I've studied people, teams, and corporate cultures, I've learned that the most innovative people in the world all follow the same process, whether they realize it or not. And this is the five-step process that they follow:

1. **Observe.** Innovators start out by observing the world around them. There are so many times when we shut down and focus on what we have in front of us. But it's when we stop, make time to be mindful, and take in what goes on around us that we start to look at the world from a different perspective.

2. **Distill.** They look at their observations, and they begin to notice patterns. It's these patterns that they distill into a broader theme.

3. **Relate.** They then do something that I call a brand transplant. They take the pattern that they've distilled from another idea and transplant that into their own brand. The ability to relate outside ideas into their own world is almost second nature. This step is key in connecting the dots between the world around them and the work that they do

4. **Generate.** Ideas generated from inspiration are powerful. People come to the table with lackluster or unrealistic ideas because they don't have a process that allows them to draw on a portfolio of experiences that have meaning to them. Or they don't know how to bring those ideas back to their own brand.

5. **Pitch.** Bad pitches kill great ideas. Every great idea needs support to go somewhere, and it's the pitch that moves a Perpetual Innovator's

work to the next level. Great pitches paint a picture and tell the story of an idea and how to realize its potential.

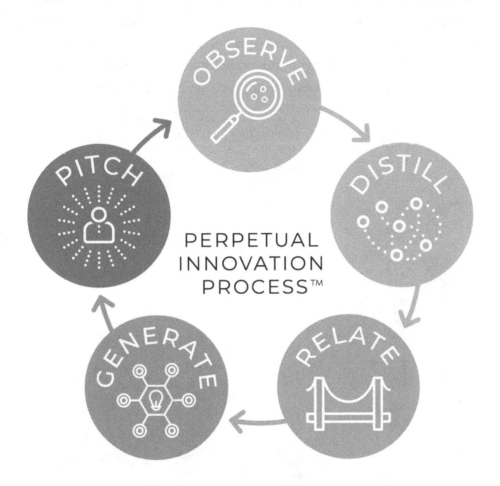

PERPETUAL INNOVATION PROCESS™

I hear too many people say they don't have good ideas, or they don't know how to come up with them. That's not true. Everyone has ideas. We've just been taught that we're not the kind of person who comes up with them. That there's a "type" of person who's smart enough, educated enough, educated in the right way, or has the right title, and they're the ones we need to trust with new ideas. Don't leave ideas to chance, we're groomed to believe—leave them to professionals with data and degrees.

It's important that everyone in your organization—no matter how big or small it is, how old or new it is, or what kind of industry you're in—learns to connect the dots between life around you and the work you do. Learning a process to come up with, vet, and share ideas can be used to solve all kinds of problems whether you're at work or home. You'll find the idea-generation process you learn helpful not only to add potential to your career but to make life more rich, exciting, and fun. Infinite opportunities come with new ideas.

CHAPTER 3

Setting Objectives

T im Washer had an impossible task on his hands.

He was the creative director of the Service Provider Market-ing Group at Cisco, and it was time to ramp up for another product launch. An engineering-driven company that sells telecommunications equip-ment, Cisco liked content that bled facts. The company's engineers loved their products. And the only thing they love more than their products was talking about them in painful detail.

A few months earlier, Tim received a request to prepare the usual "talking head" video and accompanying marketing materials to launch Cisco's new product, the ASR 9000 router switch—essentially, a metal box full of wires. He thought about gathering the usual suspects in a conference room and having a brainstorming session to come up with ideas. To bring more creativity to the table and try something new. But he's also been in enough corporate meetings to know what comes out of them: nothing that's either innovative *or* creative. Tim knew potential buyers would never simply read a press release, a web page, or watch a talking-head video of a product engineer swooning over the latest design and decide to spend hundreds of thousands of dollars on a piece of equipment.

Then one Saturday night he found himself in a comedy club in New York City. The marquee featured Ray Romano, one of the greatest comedians of all time. In the cramped, hot audience, Tim watched from his seat as Ray stood bathed in the spotlight, going through his routine. The audience roared with laughter as they wiped tears from their eyes. Line after line hit home with Ray's stories about spouses, in-laws, and kids…the kinds of things that people in the audience could directly relate to.

Tim also happens to be a stand-up comedian who's worked with the best of the best in the industry. He wrote Amy Poehler's "Weekend Update" skits on *Saturday Night Live*. When Conan O'Brien needed a crooked politician or a drunk executive, Tim got the call. He went head-to-head over climate change in a skit with Bill Nye (the Science Guy) on *Last Week Tonight* with John Oliver.

That's when Tim had a burst of brilliance for his product launch. He thought about what made Ray so relatable to people in the comedy club: he got the audience to laugh.

"If you can get someone to laugh, that builds an immediate and intimate connection," Tim said. "It makes people lower their emotional walls, and they let you in. And that's when you can begin to build a relationship with them."

Tim took this idea of comedy and getting people to laugh and connected the dots to his work in creating a video for the product launch. The Cisco ASR 9000 router would be released just before Valentine's Day. Instead of the same boring announcement, he used the idea of comedy to build a relationship with buyers.

In the opening of the video, a man's voice asks, "How many ways can a man tell his sweetheart I love you?" As the video explains, until now there were three: He could buy her expensive diamonds. He could take her on a tropical vacation. Or he could carve their initials into a tree, and then carve a heart around them. But now, he could give her the ultimate expression of his everlasting affection: the Cisco ASR 9000 router. Tim then had fun with explaining how the features of the router underscore a man's love for his sweetheart. The last scene declares that with the new Cisco router, there are now four ways for a man to express his love. While the message of the video was so ridiculous, his over-the-top approach made people laugh.

Tim didn't start out with a goal of getting analyst attention and mainstream media coverage. But that's exactly what the video generated. The *New York Times* coverage said, "In my experience, a discussion about large back-haul capacity stands as a surefire way to kill a romantic mood. And yet here's Cisco Systems arguing that such talk will win over your loved one on Valentine's Day." Industry press covered it, and that made customers look at it. The video made it easier for salespeople to talk about the new Cisco ASR 9000 router because customers were already laughing at the video. To an engineer, it was the height of appreciation for a job well done.

For Tim, all of these elements fell perfectly into place because he had a clear objective for a problem he needed to solve. When inspiration struck, his mind kicked into rapid-fire mode and connected the dots for everything he needed.

Goals versus Objectives

It turns out that the best ideas in the world come from exactly the same place that they did for Tim—everyday life. In this case, he knew exactly the problem he was looking to solve—a more creative way to launch a boring-as-all-get-out product. Knowing that, he was like a satellite in constant receive mode. Everything he took in was filtered for its potential to help him solve his problem.

As you learn the Perpetual Innovation Process and get the hang of it, you'll start with an objective and then set out to find inspiration in the world. But as you become well versed, most likely you'll start with the first step—Observe—and find an objective at a later time. Both approaches work, but which one you use depends on your dot-connecting sophistication.

One thing I want to point out is the difference between goals and objectives.

Goals are broad in scope and create the big picture of where you hope to land down the line. This means you define the destination at which you want to arrive. Goals create your focus and help you know which tactics will take you there. For example, you may have a goal to save more money this year. That's pretty vague and doesn't outline a plan for how you'll get there. They may follow a formula—e.g., SMART—but that doesn't work for open-ended innovation.

Tim's goal was to increase the number of people who reached out to a Cisco salesperson about the new ASR 9000 router.

Objectives, on the other hand, lay out the specific steps you'll take to accomplish your goal. It's all about the tactical plan you'll take to get to your destination. Objectives give you elbow room for figuring things out and making adjustments along the way. They allow you to find dots to connect, while goals try to hand them to you. If your goal is to save more money this year, then your objective may be to cut back on the number of times you eat out each month so you can put $1,000 out of every paycheck toward your retirement plan.

In Tim's situation, his objective was specific. He wanted to bring awareness to Cisco's new product launch by capturing the attention of the media and industry analysts all with a zero public relations budget.

Goals

Results   **Objectives**

The Formula for Setting Objectives

Coming up with objectives to help you hit goals is a skill everyone needs to get better at. But we don't want to fall into the trap of defaulting to the same things we've always done. If we can start with an objective that makes us stand out in new and creative ways, that's where the real money's at. In fact, the difference between people who have ideas and the ones who successfully execute them is understanding the problem that will propel business forward. If that's not the case, then your idea is a "nice to have" that will never get traction—it's new and great, but not reliable. This is because the people you need to support you will always have bigger priorities.

> The difference between people who have ideas and the ones who successfully execute them is understanding the problem that will propel the business forward.

Having an objective to work *toward* gives purpose and structure to the ideas you come up with. The purpose of your objective statement is to decide what problem you want to solve and how it bubbles up to your goal, and then align people around the work that needs to get done—all while thinking just a little bit differently.

There are three parts to the objective statement for the Perpetual Innovation process:

1. **We need new ideas to...** You need to clearly identify what you intend to work on, so your attention isn't scattered all over the place. Pick something that is big enough to make a difference but small enough to manage.

2. **So we can...** Regardless of what area of business you work in, you have to understand what specific impact you expect to make and how you'll contribute to business goals—not just marketing goals.

3. **With these constraints...** Let's face it, everything would be possible if the sky's the limit. But you have to be realistic. What constraints do you need to work with? Budget? Time? Power-hungry Kevin in

accounting who vetoes everything? List at least two that you know you'll need to work with.

In Tim's situation, he needed new ideas to bring awareness to earn 10 tweets from identified industry analysts and reporters so he could gain awareness for the Cisco ASR 9000 router all with zero PR budget.

Here are examples of other objective statements:

- We need new ideas…to differentiate our customer experience
- So we can…decrease customer churn by 5 percent
- With these constraints…within the next six months and for a budget of $1,000,000 or less

- We need new ideas…for how we conduct global employee culture training
- So we can…improve employee engagement and retention by 10 percent
- With these constraints…within the next 12 calendar months and for a budget of $500,000 or less

Now it's your turn. Fill in the blanks below to create *your* objective statement:

We need new ideas to _____

_____

So we can _____

_____

With these constraints _____

_____

This statement will ultimately serve as your North Star when you start to filter through ideas and decide which are better than others.

Anchoring the Perpetual Innovation Process

If you want more ideas that are better, inspired ideas, then you need to start looking in unconventional places. You must start looking in places different from your typical work environment, that fall out of the norm for your regular approach to your work.

Steve Jobs once said that creative people feel a bit silly when asked how they came up with a great idea. It all seems so simple to them, because it's just a process of connecting dots. What you're ultimately about to do is find a method to connect dots back to your objective in a way that you wouldn't normally do.

Now that you've articulated your objective, you're ready to begin the Perpetual Innovation process.

But beware—the first two steps feel counterintuitive because they don't tie directly to your objective. It's crucial that you take your newly formed objective and put it on the shelf for a little bit. You'll use it to make sure you're clear about the outcome for which you're looking, but you have to set it aside, so it doesn't cloud your judgment as you go through the early discovery stages.

If you're working through this process by yourself, pick an objective that you have control over, meaning you don't have to depend on other people to execute it. Maybe you need new ideas to make your board of directors meeting more entertaining so you can increase attendance by 10 percent, You only have $1,000 left in the budget, and the meeting is in two weeks. Creating clarity around anything you do by yourself will increase your chances of success.

If you're part of a team, either as a member or the leader, then you have an opportunity to think bigger. Consider how your objective could inspire your team and help them all share a common vision. Maybe you're tired of all the infighting or simply the inefficiency of meetings. Articulating your objective aligns teams and is the first step forward in creating extraordinary outcomes.

CHAPTER 4

Step 1—Observe: Collecting Dots

P eople don't always do what's good for them. While something may
make logical sense, taking action is another story all together.

That's what Dave Daigle was up against.

As the associate director for communications for public health preparedness and response for the Centers for Disease Control and Prevention
(CDC), Dave oversaw a four-person team that had a tough job: informing
the American public on how to stay safe during health emergencies like hur-
ricanes and earthquakes. Past experience showed that people who prepared
were much better off than those who don't. They were already in the midst
of a busy season—a catastrophic tornado had already hit Joplin, Missouri,
killing 158 people, injuring more than 1,100 others, and causing $2.8 billion
in damage.

One afternoon Dave and two of his colleagues, Catherine Jamal and
Maggie Silver, were in his office brainstorming ideas for campaign themes.
They wanted to take dry, factual information and package it in a way to make

people pay attention. They had no budget to work with, a stagnant web page—not even a site—and a blog.

That's when Catherine remembered something. Activity on the CDC's Twitter account, @CDCEmergency, had spiked after the meltdown at the Fukushima Daiichi nuclear plant in Japan that March. When that happened, they posted a tweet asking what emergencies people were prepared for. They were surprised with the response: zombies.

The reference hadn't come from left field. In 2010, the AMC series *The Walking Dead* premiered, and it immediately became a hit. The show followed the survivors of a zombie apocalypse trying to stay alive in the midst of near constant attacks by flesh-eating zombies. In the season finale, survivors took refuge in the CDC headquarters before it was blown up. The topic set off a craze of additional merchandise—DVD sales, video games, comic books, zombie walks, conventions, and even art. By 2011, financial news site 24/7 Wall St. estimated the zombie economy was worth billions of dollars.

The CDC team connected the dots between what people cared about and their need to make emergency preparedness interesting. That's how Dave and his team came up with the idea for their new campaign: how to prepare for a zombie apocalypse.

"We're a government entity, and we're not known for innovation or being cutting edge," Dave said. But the team felt it was worth a try.

The triad also decided to target a younger demographic, one that government agencies often ignored. "We thought if we could make inroads with younger demographics, we could get kids to ask their parents if they were prepared," explained Dave. "We were hoping that the parents would be embarrassed to say they hadn't made plans and take action."

But first, Dave had to get approval to move forward. He ran the idea past his boss, assistant surgeon general Dr. Ali Khan, who liked it and said to send him something more concrete. This is how Dave started off his email to Ali:

> I recognize this is a strange subject line. Consider how many times you have been told to stock canned goods and three days of water as well as flashlights, etc. in your home for preparedness—that is such

a tired message. Now imagine if we launched a Zombie Preparedness Campaign (tongue in cheek) saying those same messages (which would make sense if/when zombies attack). Zombies are incredibly hot and I think this would take off.

Then the team infused the preparedness message with the humor of the fictional situation. They wanted to keep the accuracy of the underlying message and what and how to prepare but overlay a story line with a more interesting potential, especially for teens and young adults. They also planned to show up where this demographic hung out: social media. It was quick and easy and fit their nonexistent budget.

The CDC team didn't have high-level metrics they were trying to hit. In fact, they didn't have a budget, they didn't set measurable goals, and they didn't outline how they were going to evaluate the work they set out to do. In asking for approval, Dave explained the situation very simply based on the timing of the season:

> Our goal is to engage this audience (one we have not engaged previously) on emergency preparedness and what steps they might take to prepare for an all hazards threat. We link and point to established tool kits, websites, and Red Cross and CDC guidance. We have an excellent window to leverage an all hazards campaign given the current flooding and a fast-approaching hurricane season. Ideally, we might draw mainstream media attention to this campaign and reach additional audiences.

Dave didn't need to jump through a lot of hoops to get the OK to start the campaign. At the time, every center had its own communications team, and the only approval he needed for the project was Ali's. Ali didn't need or seek approval from anyone else, so Dave published the first blog post on Monday, May 16, 2011, and linked it to CDC's emergency preparedness and response home page. He also sent the link to prominent news media organizations such as the *New York Times,* the *Wall Street Journal,* and CNN.

Preparedness 101: Zombie Apocalypse

Posted on May 16, 2011 by Ali S. Khan

The byline credit went to Ali, and the cheeky blog post was infused with practical information about how to prepare for a disaster. The big-picture message was that if you prepared for a zombie apocalypse, you were prepared for any emergency. The Preparedness 101: Zombie Apocalypse post began like this:

> There are all kinds of emergencies out there that we can prepare for. Take a zombie apocalypse for example. That's right, I said z-o-m-b-i-e a-p-o-c-a-l-y-p-s-e. You may laugh now, but when it happens you'll be happy you read this, and hey, maybe you'll even learn a thing or two about how to prepare for a *real* emergency.

"We were worried," Dave confided. "We knew we were skating on thin ice. As the associate director of communications, I don't have to seek clearance to post a blog. We published it and figured that if no one yelled at us or threatened to fire us, that would be our test."

When the waters remained calm, the communication team sent a tweet about the blog post and posted about it on Facebook two days later.

CDC Emergency Preparedness and Response shared a link.

Preparedness 101: Zombie Apocalypse - CDC Public Health Matters Blog
blogs.cdc.gov

There are all kinds of emergencies out there that we can prepare for. Take a zombie apocalypse for example. That's right, I said z-o-m-b-i-e a-p-o-c-a-l-y-p-s-e. You may laugh now, but when it happens you'll be happy you read this, and hey, maybe you'll even learn a thing or two about how to prepare...

Like · Comment · Share · May 18, 2011 at 10:11am ·

65 people like this.

View all 14 comments

Write a comment...

That's when things got crazy!

A typical blog post might range between 1,000 to 3,000 hits. But once the team promoted the article, traffic surged so drastically that the server crashed nine minutes after the first tweet. It had 60,000 hits by Thursday and was a trending topic on Twitter.

"Public health and preparedness are not sexy. But it turns out, zombies are," Dave said.

Sticking with their spend-no-money budget, the team focused on digital media to offer buttons, badges, and widgets for people to use on websites, blogs, social media profiles, and email signatures. They followed up a few months later with posters and magnets. The CDC Foundation, a nonprofit that supports the CDC, began selling Zombie Task Force T-shirts online. By October, several people had emailed the CDC suggesting they create a graphic novella. So, Maggie wrote up a 34-page version that combined a fictional horror story with a practical guide on how to prepare for any emergency.

PREPAREDNESS 101:

ZOMBIE PANDEMIC

CDC — U.S. Department of Health and Human Services Centers for Disease Control and Prevention

In response to public requests, the CDC created a graphic novella that combined a fictional zombie apocalypse storyline with a practical guide on how to prepare for any emergency.

Because of the popularity of the campaign, Ali was invited to speak at Comic Con in New York City and Dragon Con in Atlanta. That's right. Comic Con invited a top official from the CDC to speak about public health.

"Zombies have been a really good way to get people to engage with preparedness…It served as a great bridge to talk about public health in general," Ali explained. "All of a sudden, people are willing to hear about public health and how interesting it is, because we've mixed it with something they already want to hear about, zombies."

In a short amount of time, Dave, Maggie, and Catherine earned tremendous attention for a previously invisible subject: emergency preparedness.

- The CDC's emergency preparedness and response website traffic increased by 1,143 percent in 2011 compared with 2010.
- The first tweet on May 18 prompted 70,426 clicks and generated 34,714 unique tweets.
- Twitter generated more than 1.1 million views of the blog post.
- The @CDCEmergency feed gained more than 11,000 followers.
- The department's Facebook page gained more than 7,000 fans in the three weeks following the blog post.
- The comic book has been viewed more than 517,600 times.
- The CDC distributed more than 18,500 zombie apocalypse posters.

The campaign generated massive national and international media attention. More than 3,000 articles and news broadcasts were published or aired during the first week alone, reaching an estimated 3.6 million people. The campaign was admitted into the PR Hall of Fame along with works from brands like Coca-Cola.

This extraordinarily successful campaign cost a total of $87—the cost of the graphic used in the May 11, 2011, blog post.

Think Like a Kid

The interesting thing about Dave, Maggie, and Catherine is that you don't expect this kind of observation from adults. We simply don't make connections between things that are drastically different and come up with something new.

But we did when we were kids.

When we were little, we noticed everything around us. We paid attention to the smallest detail. Ants carrying bits of dirt one-by-one. How ice cream melts and runs down the side of a cone. Shapes we see in clouds. As an adult, we have a heightened sense of what kids notice, more so than we did as one our self. Perhaps one of the most humbling is when we hear our words come out of their mouth. They've carefully watched every detail of how we behave, and then model that behavior.

My mother is still horrified over me doing this exact thing.

When I was four, I was over the moon to be in the community fashion show. Now, I grew up in a town of 1,000 people in rural Nebraska, so this was the local equivalent of fashion week in Paris, Milan, or New York.

My mother had stayed up nearly half the night making sure the matching dresses my sister and I wore were close to perfection. With my long blond hair in curls, I looked at my short white socks and black-patent Mary Jane shoes. I smoothed the skirt of my navy-blue dress with its red and white polka dots as one of the ladies from church shared her admiration for my outfit.

I was delighted and felt quite mature as I let her in on a little secret: "My momma poke her finger. Her say…dammit!"

I glanced at my mother with pride in being part of a mature conversation and felt puzzled as to why her face suddenly reddened. She abruptly turned the other direction and made faux adjustments to my sister's dress.

This ability to observe starts at a very young age. Babies do something called mouthing to learn about the world around them. This form of oral exploration is an important part of their development, because it's by putting toys and other objects in their mouth that they discover tastes and textures. The dead beetle in the backyard. The piece of fuzz on the floor. A fistful of dog hair.

As they grow into toddlers and young children, they shift their observational tactics from mouthing to play. Play may sound simple, but it's an incredibly complex process through which kids learn to observe life and make use of it. It leads them to a chain of why-why-why questions that make most adults want to pull their hair out.

By the time we're adults, we've quit observing like we did as kids.

Why You Miss the Gorilla

As adults, we don't play. We go through much of our life on autopilot because we think we've seen everything. There's also a demand for efficiency.

I know I've been guilty of driving from one place to another and not remembering a thing about the trip. It was a route I took so often that my mind was busy trying to solve other problems on my to-do list. Like you, I pass mentally unconscious through repetitive parts of my life and don't even remember them. Autopilot lets us keep up with the demands of our existence, but there's a cost to it. We miss seeing important elements in the world that can turn into fodder for brilliant ideas.

There's a scientific term for this: inattentional blindness. This happens when you're so wrapped up in one thing—e.g., your cell phone—that you don't notice something else that's obvious and right in front of you.

And by obvious, I mean really obvious.

For more than a decade, Daniel Simons has studied inattentional blindness. He's a professor in the Departments of Psychology, Advertising, and Business Administration at the University of Illinois. His work looks at the limits of human perception, memory, and awareness. Daniel's best known for his research showing that people are far less aware of their visual surroundings than they think.

In 2010, Daniel and his colleague Christopher Chabris published a book called *The Invisible Gorilla*. In it, they share stories and counterintuitive scientific findings to reveal an important truth: Our minds don't work the way we think they do. We think we see ourselves and the world as they actually are, but in truth we miss a whole lot.

In their research, Daniel and Chris had volunteers watch a 60-second video in which two groups of people passed around basketballs. One group wore white shirts and the other black. Then, they asked the participants to count the number of passes the players dressed in white made and ignore the people dressed in black.

Here's the experiment part: While the observers were busy counting passes, a woman in a full-body gorilla suit walked into the center of the frame, pounded her chest, and walked off. Unbelievably, about half the people who took the test never even saw the woman in the gorilla suit. Some of those who didn't see the gorilla protested that the video had been rigged. People who did see her were in disbelief: How could so many miss something so obvious?

Daniel and Chris had stumbled onto a basic lapse in human visual perception: inattentional blindness, the failure to see something blatantly obvious when you focus your attention on something else.

The video became an internet sensation.

Daniel and Chris used the idea of the invisible gorilla to explain why a company would spend billions to launch a product that its own analysts know will fail. How a lifeguard could run right past someone waving and yelling for help without seeing them. Why award-winning movies are full of editing mistakes.

Every day you think you see the world as it is, but in truth, so much goes on that you're never even aware of. You mow through a bag of chips while watching a movie and don't remember the second bite. You drive to work and don't remember even backing out of the driveway. You put your kids to bed and can't remember kissing them goodnight. Societies write traffic laws and build criminal cases on the assumption that people will notice when something unusual happens right in front of them. But that's not how we operate.

Developing Awareness

When we get off the beaten path, even just a little bit, that all changes. Travel to a new country—or even a new city—and the details of everything heightens all of your senses. You smell all the smells, hear all the sounds, feel the change in temperature, see how people behave differently, and taste different flavors. Rent a car and drive in Oslo and compare how that feels to driving in Omaha. Play fútbol in Madrid and compare that to football in Mumbai. Eat dinner in Bethlehem and compare that to Buenos Aires.

When you report back to friends and family about your experience, you recreate even the smallest details. What it's like to circle a roundabout (again) in Europe. Fútbol and football are two completely different sports. And you made sure to eat everything on your plate in Tokyo.

It's at times like these, when you're in the midst of something completely unfamiliar, that you're most likely to go back to those childhood patterns. You pay attention to every detail, watch what's going on, and pause to take in the sights, sounds, smells, textures, and tastes of what you're experiencing.

Let me explain what I mean.

Mindfulness, Observation, and Innovation

On the surface, observation appears to be a simple skill. But as we can see from the invisible gorilla experiment, it's more complex than we would imagine.

Part of the reason observation is hard is because your mind runs at a thousand miles a second. Even as you're reading this sentence, you're thinking about having to pick up the dry cleaning, how to get the dog puke stain out of the carpet, and whether or not you'll have to see your mother-in-law at the holidays. You've let society train your brain into constant distraction. This adds to your inattentional blindness.

You cure this with mindfulness.

Mindfulness is a mental state in which your awareness is fully on the present moment. You're not thinking about this afternoon's meeting or last night's football score. It means maintaining a moment-by-moment awareness of your thoughts, feelings, bodily sensations, and your surrounding environment. It involves acceptance, meaning that you pay attention to your thoughts and feelings without judging them—understanding that there's no right or wrong way to think or feel in a given moment.

Becoming more mindful means living in the present moment. When you live in the present moment, you're more observant of what's going on around you and you have objectivity in how you look at things. It helps you notice and appreciate the details of your surroundings.

By using mindfulness to improve your observation skills, you'll tap into your creative energy and discover nuances and details you hadn't noticed before. This will open your mind to new possibilities and help you build a repertoire of experiences that can ignite innovation.

The Perpetual Observer

Observation is the process of removing blinders and experiencing the world around you with curiosity. Making time to look at the details of your environment heightens your awareness and makes you sensitive to things you'd normally find mundane. It gives meaning to the minutiae.

You may not realize it, but you observe things and connect dots all day long. "Dots" are small specks of observations that you accumulate over time.

You see your U2 concert T-shirt, remember Bono is Irish, and decide to get fish and chips for dinner. You get something out of your trunk, see the jumper cables, and remember you need to batteries for the smoke alarm. Or, on your morning run, you notice a bird adding twigs to a nest and remember you need to clean the gutters.

Every person has the ability to acquire and connect dots. But while everyone does this without realizing it, natural innovators consciously practice it. They understand they have the ability to find inspiration for a great idea in any situation. Henry Ford got the idea for his assembly line from a meatpacking plant. Swiss engineer George de Mestral was inspired to invent Velcro after seeing his dog covered in prickly burrs. And Mercedes-Benz designers found inspiration in the two-door compact car-shaped boxfish for one of its aerody-

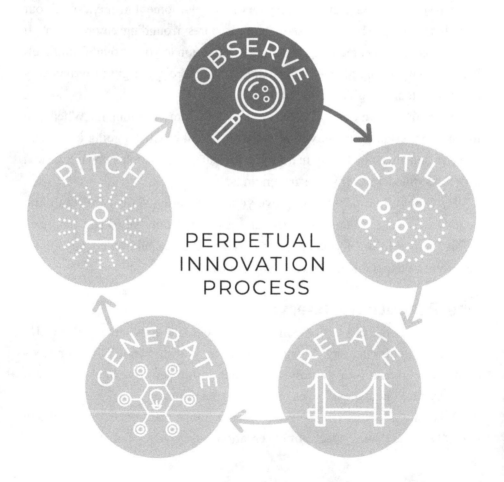

namic models. These innovators consciously and purposefully connected the dots rather than dismissing experiences as random interactions. Henry Ford knew he was looking for a new process to assemble cars, and he sought out opportunities to learn from other markets and situations. That's what led him to learn about the meatpacking industry and tour a plant.

As you begin the first step of the Perpetual Innovation process—Observe— you will begin curing your blindness by working on situational observation and awareness skills. Learning to observe means learning to pay attention to what you see, smell, hear, taste, and touch. It heightens your awareness of mundane, everyday things because you experience them with a fresh perspective. Success comes when you remove the judgment about what's important and what's not. Your goal in learning how to become a better observer is to learn to pay attention with an open mind, collect "dots" through your senses, and begin to stockpile what you experience in the world around you.

Keep this in mind, though. When you set out to observe the world around you, the more you change up your environment, the better you'll get. Just like when you step out of your comfort zone when you travel, diverse stimuli raise your awareness. The more diverse the places and situations you put yourself in, the more diverse your observations. Since our goal is to learn how to better connect the dots, I'll call the observations you collect "dots."

If you're going to practice this observation exercise five times in a week, then pick five really different places. Or, if you're going to do this once a week for the next five months, pick various locations each time. An opera house, a neighborhood basketball court, a university student center, a train station, the back 40 on a farm, or a wax museum. I once spent an hour and a half in a coffee shop in the arrivals area of the Barcelona airport making observations. Then the next day I sat along a marsh in the foothills doing the same thing while my brother went bird-watching.

This may seem boring and tedious, but think about this. For anyone to experience consistent growth, they keep a logbook of their progress. Athletes keep a fitness journal to log how far they ran, when, and in what time. Scientists keep logbooks to monitor their experiments. Pilots keep a written log of the hours they've flown. Observation is a skill just like any other. And in order to get better at it, you need to have a written log of your work to refer back to and learn from.

How to Observe: Four Steps

The practice of observing involves four steps:

1. **Watch.** What do people do? What exists? What are the individual ingredients that make up what you see, hear, taste, touch, and smell? For example, if you see a man running to catch a bus, how's he dressed? Is he old, young? Is he sprinting down the street or hobbling? Take note of his jacket, shoes, and pants; the color of his backpack; and the type of haircut he has. Is he wearing glasses? Does he get to the bus stop on time? All of these details will have meaning for your work.

2. **List.** Get a specific notebook to use for your Observation Journal. It can be as simple as a lined notebook, or you can buy something fancy that makes the time you spend observing the world feel more special. Buy a journal with cartoon characters on the front if that helps bring out the curious child in you. Then, use it to create a running inventory of everything you take in, item by item, sensation by sensation. Cold cement bench. Warm sun on your face. Hot air from the vent. Bright light from the squad car. Smelly dog poo behind the park bench. Sticky leftover ketchup on the fast-food wrapper. The shout of someone trying to get their friend's attention in the distance. Tall trees without leaves. You get the idea.

3. **Dissect.** Pick the list apart and analyze what you've come up with in detail. Do you realize you've only written down things you see, but few of what you hear and nothing that has taste? Getting down to the nitty gritty of what you've observed shows you where you have gaps and what sense you lean on first. Close your eyes and sounds will become more prevalent. Plug your ears at the same time and what you feel becomes more obvious. Your different senses send information to the brain to help you perceive your environment. When you add or subtract what one or more senses experience, you change how your brain responds to what you take in.

4. **Detail.** Give a detailed account that reveals the expanse of what you've experienced. You can talk to yourself out loud or write some notes in your Observation Journal. The key here is to help your brain bring closure to your observation exercise, or you'll find it will run on for an eternity, remembering the smallest details and making you feel they have to be added to your list. For example, you may say to yourself, "Today, at this art museum I've seen all the different paintings that Monet painted. I've heard the excitement and indifference of other visitors. The light and sound of the space has been a part of the experience. And I've detected every scent possible. I've taken in all I can, and now my exercise is complete."

Putting It into Play

As you decide where to go each time for your exercise, pack your Observation Journal. Once you're at your destination, find a comfortable place to sit. ***Put your phone away.*** The point of this exercise is to slow down and take in the world around you. You can't do that if you're checking your phone every few minutes, and you are not allowed to take notes on your phone. Now, for the next 30 minutes, watch what goes on. What kind of people do you see? What sounds do you hear? How is the area laid out? Are there smells that are unique to the place or time of day when you're there?

Don't discount anything. Take it all in. After 30 minutes your mind will have begun to relax. It's important that you give yourself this time, because you need mental space to forget about your to-do list and where you need to be next. Then, take 30 minutes and write down everything you noticed, no matter how big or small. Don't judge whether anything is relevant or not. Your assignment in this exercise is to take in as much as you can and document it, all in less than an hour.

As an example, following is a list of thinks I observed at a coffee shop by my house in Denver:

- People in line
- Food in glass case
- Microwave dings

- Smell of coffee
- Hard floor
- Skid-free rug
- Man chewing fingernails
- Woman on phone
- Man texting
- People's names on cups
- Sugar/stirrer/napkin station
- Trash can inside cabinet
- Barstools
- Tall table
- Short table
- Hard-back chairs
- Cushy chairs
- Bright lights
- Cozy corner
- Woman reading
- Laughter
- Burnt coffee smell
- Baby crying
- Poopy diaper smell
- Pastries
- Breakfast food
- Lunch food
- Snacks
- Sweetness of my hot cocoa
- Coffee to go
- Floral perfume
- Outdoor seating
- People waiting for drinks
- Hot drinks
- Cold drinks
- Feeling of sugar on the table

- Tall ceilings
- Single-gender bathrooms
- Baby-changing station
- Wall soap dispenser
- Community flyers
- Sugar packet wrappers on floor
- Straw wrappers on floor
- Crumbs on tables
- Cups with names written on them
- Cold breeze from open door
- Employee uniforms
- Menu high on wall
- Background music
- Tip jar
- Bananas
- Cooler with drinks below food case
- Pound packages of coffee to go
- Gift cards
- Used newspapers
- To-go coffee mugs for sale
- Cardboard sleeves for cups
- Overflowing trashcan
- Hugs
- Kiss

These are just some of the things I observed, and I wrote many more in my Observation Journal. It was a busy time of day—rush hour in the morning—so people and things moved quickly. It was a different experience than if I had taken an hour in the afternoon when people are more likely to linger and work or catch up with friends.

Now it's your turn. Open your Observation Journal and turn to a fresh page. Write down everything you see, hear, feel, taste, or touch. Nothing you notice is too big or too insignificant to take note of. Don't worry about whether you're doing it right or wrong (there's no such thing), or if someone sees you sitting, doing nothing, and taking notes on it. Your purpose is simply to take time to be where you are and write down everything you take in.

For your first time, shoot for at least 100 observations. As you go through the process more than five times, you'll find that you'll come up with 200–300 observations with greater ease. This is because you're teaching your brain how to pay attention. With this exercise you actually have two goals. The first is to train your brain to become more observant out of habit. The second is to collect dots (observations) to which you can refer back as we move into the next steps of the Perpetual Innovation process.

When you've done this at least five times, you'll find that your brain begins to take note of details without you needing to tell it to. You'll be in line at the grocery store, and all of a sudden you'll see things for the first time that have always been there. Maybe you're sitting on a plane and see tiny details in the pattern in the carpet in the aisle. Or you could notice inflections in people's voices that reveal hidden emotions.

The reason that practice is important is that you need to make a habit of collecting dots. This is because before you can get to having better ideas, you have to start with more ideas. And in order to have more ideas, you need to be able to make connections between as many dots as possible. As you work through the Perpetual Innovation process, you'll winnow down the things you have to work with as you go through each step. By having hundreds of observations to start with, you'll find yourself in a much better place when it's time to start generating new ideas down the line.

Until then, what do you do with all the observations you've collected so far? That's what we'll get into in the next chapter: Distill.

CHAPTER 5

Step 2—Distill: Poking for Patterns

Hiero was a tyrant who believed his goldsmith was cheating him. He didn't know how to prove it—he suspected the goldsmith was swapping out gold with silver—so he hired Archimedes, a local mathematician and engineer, to prove it for him.

This was an important assignment. The object in question was a wreath dedicated to the gods. This wasn't the kind of problem that Archimedes had come across his desk every day, and he accepted the challenge. But he needed time to think about it.

As a man of science, Archimedes was a natural observer of the world around him. On a trip to the public baths, he noticed something that turned out to be important: The more his body sank into the water, the more water he displaced. In fact, the amount of water his body displaced was exactly equivalent to the volume of his body.

Once Archimedes realized this, his brain quickly made another connection. Because gold weighed more than the same volume of silver, he reasoned that if the metals in the crown were a mix of gold and silver, it would displace more water than one made purely of gold because of the lighter weight of silver.

With a realization so great he couldn't wait to act on it, the math whiz leapt out of the bath and sprinted home naked, crying, "Eureka! Eureka!" all the way. That translates to, "I found it! I found it!"

Everyone knows this story, but they don't know the real lesson.

In mathematician terms, Archimedes of Syracuse was considered the best of the best. But it turns out, what dawned on him in the public baths is something that comes naturally to humans if we allow our brains to do what it does naturally: find patterns that lead to bigger insights.

The Ultimate Information Processor

There's no better information processing machine than the human brain. It's uncanny at how it observes things, connects the dots between what it sees, and turns those into patterns. In fact, our brain's ability to recognize patterns is an inherent trait that's wired into us—even babies are born knowing how to detect patterns.

Genetically, connecting the dots to recognize patterns have kept us alive and safe. If your prehistoric ancestors hadn't recognized patterns of safety, they wouldn't recognize the threat that breaks those patterns. As their brain constantly took note of their surroundings, it absorbed all the little details (dots) that created an environment in which they could let their guard down, a landscape they could easily scan, calm animals, and a clear sky. But when something broke that pattern—a flock of birds suddenly taking flight for no obvious reason or an unexpected rustle in the grass behind them—their brain kicked in and sent out a warning signal. They escaped danger to live another day.

Just like our ancestors, you and I observe the world around us, connect dots, and discover patterns that give meaning and clues to what we should pay attention to and what we can ignore. Perhaps things are OK down that dark alley, and you don't need to do a more detailed inspection before taking that first confident step. Or, maybe it makes sense to take another route home. The ability to quickly connect dots and come up with patterns is a timesaver.

**Connecting the dots between observations
is how your brain sees a relationship between things.**

Patterns show a consistency in which these relationships appear.

Without you even realizing it, your brain connects hundreds of dots in a microsecond as it looks for patterns. The more dots you have to connect, the more patterns you'll see. The key to being able to recognize patterns is your ability to collect more dots and then connect them in multiple ways.

Your brain's ability to process in this way is why you buy a blue car and suddenly you see blue cars everywhere. If you're an avid dot collector, your pattern recognition skills may overflow into noticing people wearing blue shirts. You'll see more blue in the magazines you read, and blue seems to be the color theme of every website you visit. Your brain connects the dots between things that are similar and finds patterns that may otherwise feel completely random.

Something interesting happens with how you detect patterns. When you consciously set out to look for them, the part of your brain you put to work the hardest to look for these connections isn't actually the part that gives you the huge eureka moments. When you put thought behind making sense of what you see in the world around you, you use linear problem solving. This means you try to solve problems by logically working out a solution. Think about adding several six-figure numbers without a calculator or doing time-zone math. This kind of thinking uses your conscious memory. These are the things you need to keep handy so you can decide where to eat lunch or find your way home from the gym.

As you go from dawn to dusk, your working memory maxes out pretty quickly. This is why you feel exhausted at the end of a demanding day. You've consciously tried to knock down one roadblock after another.

On the other side of the fence, there's the unconscious part of your brain, which tackles nonlinear problems like finding patterns.

This is actually where you do the heavy lifting in connecting the dots and coming up with insights— you just don't realize it because much of the work happens behind the scenes. The number of linear problems your brain solves in a day is infinitesimal compared with the volume of nonlinear ones. Take, for example, when your boss says you need new ways to increase customer experience scores, but there's no room in the budget to make it happen. There's no preexisting or logical solution. You may assume there's no way to make it happen, but there's part of your brain already going to work trying to figure out a way to connect dots and solve the problem.

From Dots to Constellations

Everyone who's ever looked up at the night sky has seen a group of stars. If you don't know what to look for, they just look like random blips of light. Orion, one of the most recognizable constellations in the world, is a great

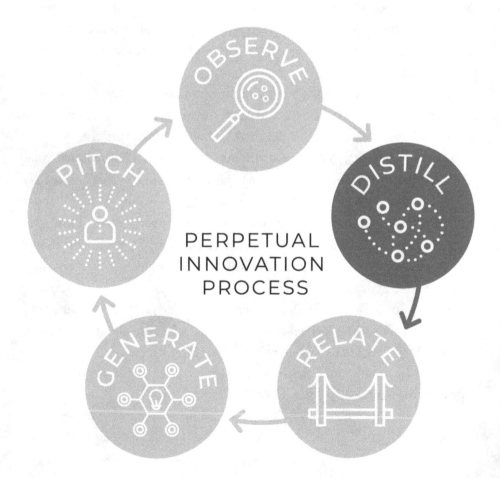

example. At first glance in that area of the sky, there's nothing that makes sense. But as you pay more attention, you'll see three stars in a row that make his belt. Two bright points depict his shoulders, and another two his knees. With just seven stars, you have before you a Greek mythological hunter. That's all constellations are: patterns of stars made up by connecting dots.

In the Observe step, you collected dots—ideally, hundreds of different types of them. The more dots (experiences) you have to start with, the more connections you'll have to draw from down the line. As you collect more and more dots, you'll begin to see how to connect them into patterns that form potential constellations.

I've spent the last few years interviewing people from all walks of life about how they came up with their own eureka moments. And it turns out, they have to stop and think hard about how they connected the dots because it comes naturally to them. In the Distill step, you'll learn how to develop your skill in connecting the dots just like they do, so that it becomes second nature for you, just like it does for them.

Distilling is the process of discovering the common and essential aspects of multiple observations and finding a broader commonality between all of them. When you distill what you've observed, it empowers you to extract value from what you experience.

The entire purpose of the Distill step is to learn how to connect dots so you can identify patterns. Observation for observation's sake isn't helpful. You need to take the essence of what you take in and distill that until you see broader themes. In the Distill step, you want to look for similarities in your observations and then put them into groups. This delays your knee-jerk reaction of wanting to jump ahead and generate ideas too soon. It slows down the creative process, which gives your brain more time and leeway to think in a nonlinear fashion.

As you work through the Distill step, keep in mind you're not getting graded on this, and there's no right or wrong answer. You aren't even looking for the *best* connections or ones that will solve your problem. The work that you do in the Distill step is actually counterintuitive. You'll feel an urge to jump ahead to the Generate step, but be patient. While it might feel that you have the key to solving your problem, trust me, you're not there yet. Actually, the secret to solving your problem is to continue to forget about your objective for a little while longer. This will slow you down long enough for me to show you how the entire process works, and why there's a reason for each step.

Let's look at how Tim Washer worked through the Perpetual Innovation Process. He spent several hours in a comedy club one night. He watched the comedians on stage, both the warm-up acts and the headliner. He savored what created the ambiance and took in the audience's reactions to the show. Slowly, he took each of his observations and began collecting others in his head. As he distilled what he observed, he saw the patterns of relating to an audience, quickly creating intimacy, and building relationships. Tim knew it was important to put his objective in the back of his mind while he let his mind do what he had trained it to do. This is the foundation of getting to better ideas once you get to the Generate step, but you can't shortchange the process before you get there.

How to Distill: Three Steps

As you evaluate your observations, you'll go through the following three steps to decide what has meaning and discover relationships to other "dots".

1. **Scrutinize.** What are all the ways in which two or more things share a common element? For example, a hipster tattoo artist with low-slung pants, a white-haired priest, and an exotic dancer may all appear drastically different. But, believe it or not, they have a lot in common. The same goes for the flagpole outside a school, the billboard advertising a new retirement community, and a radio tower on the horizon.

2. **Discern.** What meaning do these elements have in relationship to each other? This can come from the smallest of elements. For the hipster, priest, and dancer, it could be something as simple as they make a living working with other people. For the flagpole, billboard, and radio tower, maybe one of the commonalities is that they all signal something.

3. **Identify.** What are the bigger patterns that arrive from these common elements? Go through your list of observations. What patterns do you start to see? Give each grouping a label. With our example, the three people could be the start of a group called "Pleasure" or even "Sin."

For the flagpole, billboard, and radio tower, the bigger meaning could be "Communication." Then you may add in some other observations that fit the communication category, such as a stop sign, someone saying hello, and a turn signal on a car. There are no rules on what you choose to name the groups. The labels only need to reflect the spirit of the observations.

There's no level of importance to the connections you make; you're simply looking for relationships. What you observe or the patterns you find matter much less than the fact that you practice making the connections. The process itself is the goal.

The Practice

Start by writing each one of your observations on its own sticky note and place them all on a wall or a large, open flat space—someplace where you can see all of them at once. As you scan your bevvy of sticky notes, you'll begin to notice things that have similarities. Group these together and use another sticky note to give them a label. I like to use one color of note for the observation and a second for the Distill label. Some people use the same color sticky notes but use a different color marker for each stage. Regardless of how you differentiate your observations from the Distill labels, it is important that you're able to quickly tell the difference between them. As you add more steps to the process, having different colors helps you keep track of what step you're on. This proves helpful as you work with hundreds of sticky notes. (If you're going through the Perpetual Innovation Process with a remote team in a virtual environment, you can use an online tool such as Mural.)

For example, once I wrote all of my observations from my morning at the coffee shop on sticky notes, a few began to stand out as having similar traits:

- Man chewing fingernails. I didn't like the thought of all the places his hands had been before he put them in his mouth to chew his fingernails. And I was certain that he either spit them out or swallowed them after he bit them off. Both made my stomach curdle thinking about it.

- Poopy diaper smell. If you've ever smelled a poopy diaper…just…ick.
- Trash on floor. I watched people half-heartedly put their cups and napkins in the overstuffed trash cans, only to have them spill out on the floor. There were pools of coffee sticky with sugar that I could see caught dirt from people's shoes. The stickiness and dirt got tracked into other areas of the coffee shop and made the floor a mess.
- Burnt coffee smell. It wasn't just a little burnt; this was a pot that someone clearly forgot about during a rush and it boiled dry. It was so strong that some customers came through the door, took a whiff, and then turned on their heels.
- Crumbs on table. This one's an attention to detail element. No one came around to clean up the table. I set my mug of coffee down only to have the bottom covered with crumbs from someone else's break-fast. Who knows if it fell from the muffin itself or out of their mouth? I tried not to think too much about it.

As my eyes caught these observations, I scrutinized their common elements, discerned the meaning that they had to each other, and identified a bigger pattern. I labeled this Distill category "Icky Things."

If you were looking at my observations, your background and experience may lead you to connect the dots in different ways. You may add things such as perfume, feeling of sugar on the table, and community flyer on this same list. This could be because perfume makes you nauseous, sugar on the table makes you think the coffee shop as a whole isn't clean, and you find community events super frustrating. However, if you find these things pleasant, or at least not icky, you put them on different lists.

There's no rhyme or reason to how you label your Distill groups; it's what makes sense to you (or your group, if you're going through the exercise as a team). You might notice that some observations fit into more than one category. For example, the man chewing his fingernails could also go into a category you label as "habits." That's OK; just make another sticky note and put it in as many categories as you'd like. As you group your observations together and label them, it will begin to look something like this.

Here's an example of another group of observations in which I found a pattern:

- Cushy chairs. I *love* sitting in a big, soft, cushy chair in a coffee shop and just relaxing. I've even been known to doze off. These chairs definitely put me in my comfort zone.

- Background music. Something loud enough to hear, but soft enough that it doesn't get in the way of good conversation. It makes a busy place feel less like a business and more like my living room.

- People's names on cups. Who doesn't like a personalized touch? Having someone see me often enough to remember my name so I don't have to give it to them makes me feel like we're friends.

- Community flyer. I'm a small-town girl. I love seeing what's going on in the community around me. It makes me feel more connected to the area in which I live.

- Laughter. I grew up in a house full of hilarity. There are few things that make me feel more at home than hearing someone else enjoying a good belly laugh.

- Hugs. That's right up there with laughter. If we ever meet, know that I'm a hugger.

As I scrutinize and discern my observations so I can identify patterns, I decide to label this group of dots "Comfort." This Distill category now looks like this:

If you feel stuck with this step, you're overthinking things. This exercise is *way* simpler than you realize…but it's not easy. This is when your complexity bias kicks in and you'll feel you need to make this more complicated than it needs to be. Relax. The power in this step truly comes from the simplicity of it.

Give Constellations Credibility

We now know that humans are programmed to see patterns and interpret them in ways that have meaning. This is both good and bad. As you grow up, you learn to organize things in ways that make sense to you. As you become more efficient with recognizing them, it helps keep you from feeling overwhelmed when you take in a lot of stimulation at once. You learn what to pay attention to and what to ignore. When you ignore too much, you become blind to the inspiration that's all around you.

Great insights really can pop out of nowhere. But to have that happen, you have to first practice connecting dots and then make use of them by identifying their patterns. In the next step, Relate, you'll learn how your constellations move from theory and begin to have context in the real world.

CHAPTER 6

Step 3—Relate: Transplanting Inspiration

A s Ben Bacal grew up in Toronto, Canada, he dreamed of a life working in the film industry in Hollywood. At 17, he left home and moved to Los Angeles to study film and electronic arts at California State University, Long Beach.

After he graduated, he went to work for Sony and Warner Bros. Studios, creating special effects. He loved his work, but his heart was one step ahead of him—he wanted to produce his own films.

Ben didn't make a lot of money as special effects guy. Or at least the kind of money he needed to produce his own work. He started to look around for something else he could do to supplement his income. His mom had been a real estate agent back in Toronto, so he thought he'd take a look at real estate.

In studying the industry, he observed something about how real estate agents marketed their services—it was pretty static. And pretty awful. They plastered their faces on park benches and bus stops. They sent out a lot of postcards that people promptly threw out. And then they sat back and waited for the phone to ring.

It was 2005, and Ben was an ambitious 24-year-old. His first problem was to figure out how to market himself. He started by going house to house, knocking on people's front doors. When they answered, he introduced himself and said he had a buyer for their house. Had they ever considered selling? If they said yes, he scrambled to find a buyer. Believe it or not, it worked. Really well.

In his first year as an agent, Ben sold $17 million in real estate. His commission: $394,000. It sounds like a lot of money, but if you're looking to finance Hollywood movies, it takes a bigger pool of cash than that.

That's when Ben thought back to his first love: film. He observed that movies have the power to take people places they never imagined. To transport them to another time and place. To provoke emotions and get people to pay attention. This is how studios created ardent fans that waited with bated breath for their next release. And why people were willing to pay more for work that some directors produced than others.

Noodling on his observations, he distilled a pattern behind it all. Film was a way to get people to pretend. To see themselves in ways they never imaged before. Movies were also a way to build a large audience of passionate fans.

As he thought about his work, Ben asked himself a question. What if he could use the same approach to get people to pretend—to transport them into the home of their dreams—while building an audience for his real estate business?

That was the spark of inspiration Ben needed. He started shooting videos with his iPhone of the properties he listed—or even someone else's—edited them, and uploaded them to YouTube, Facebook, and even Myspace. While Ben could knock on 20–30 doors a week, an online video got 100 hits in a day or over a 1,000 in a week. Video was his opportunity to scale his outreach.

Next, Ben added content pieces about the neighborhood and agent profiles about himself. He found that the videos showing his face and walking through a property performed much better than those that just showed the listing. By seeing Ben in the picture, it was easier for buyers to see themselves in any potential new house.

Elaborate videos have now become Ben's trademark. He'll take a regular listing and turn the real estate videos into property dramas. He's created them just like he would a Hollywood film, which have characters, a suspenseful plot, and stars.

For example, the *Hollywood Reporter* describes one video like this: "Dusk in the Hollywood Hills, A melancholy piano fills the soundtrack with Debussy's haunting 'Clair de Lune.' The camera focuses on a man in a blue blazer as he enters a stunning glass-box-style modern house. He heads straight into the sleek all-white kitchen and pours himself a tumbler of booze from a crystal decanter. Then he strolls onto the wrap-around terrace and stares moodily at the city lights for a bit until climbing upstairs to the spacious master bedroom, where he encounters his wife applying makeup in their enormous luxury bathroom. 'I want a divorce,' he tells her, delivering the line so woodenly he'd have Keanu Reeves slapping his forehead."

While it may not be Oscar-worthy acting, it's killer marketing. This 10-minute mini movie is part of a soon-to-be divorced couple's $4.5 million property listing. The owners are the stars, and as the plot takes them through their argument and inevitable marital split, viewers see the details of the space and high-tech amenities. (Plot twist…the couple isn't *actually* getting a divorce.)

Ben was one of the first people in his industry to use video for all of his real estate marketing. With it, he went from being an average producer in his office to selling over $2 billion in properties. He estimates that his videos have been a boon to his business in the range of "a thousandfold." In 2013, he started using drones to shoot video of properties. He put together montages of clips for some properties and uploaded them to YouTube. One of them went viral and reached a Dutch technology developer who wanted to buy a home in Los Angeles. Part of Ben's current notoriety is his status as the agent for the most expensive listing in the United States, located in Bel Air, California, for $250 million. In fact, he has created such a strong brand for himself that when word gets out that he's listed a home in a neighborhood, the average property value actually goes up.

It's been a long road from knocking door to door, looking for listings, to becoming one of the top real estate agents in the United States. He's now in a position to go back to the Hollywood film industry, but there's no need.

Why?

He wanted to make high-quality feature films. He's doing that. A few of his productions cost $20,000 to make, but that's chump change compared with the $20 million price tag on some of his client's homes. Ben wanted to work with A-list actors. He can check that box, too, having bought or sold homes for the likes of Ellen DeGeneres, Madonna, and Matt Damon.

Why did Ben's approach of marrying Hollywood movies with selling high-end real estate work? It's because he was able to relate blockbuster films to his work as an agent before he asked, "How do I sell more houses?" If Ben had asked, "How do I apply movie techniques to sell houses?," I guarantee he wouldn't have been as successful. His work would have come across as cheesy or trying to copycat big-name studios. Instead, he observed what happened when films became box office hits—they attracted a lot of attention, created a buzz, and generated intrigue. Next he connected the dots and distilled them into a pattern—Hollywood movies created groups of fans, followers who moved from one piece of work to another. He realized that's exactly what he wanted to do in the real estate business. Ben wanted to create a fan base of his work, so people would come see his listings. The more eyeballs he attracted, the more likely he was to sell a property. And more viewers mean a greater demand, which boosts the price. Both Hollywood studios and real estate agents need to attract attention, create a buzz, and generate intrigue. Ben had the realization he could do for real estate what movies do for Hollywood.

That's why Ben's idea worked. He observed the world around him and distilled it into a pattern, and now he related Hollywood movie success to his work as a real estate agent. It's the *process* he used that made his idea successful. This point of relating inspiration from another source to his own work is also the critical point at which most innovation efforts fail. The temptation is that once you observe something successful and distill it into a pattern, you jump into the objective and start generating ideas without taking time to fully understand the first two steps. The Relate step creates the critical space to contextualize your thinking that increases the chances of success.

Conducting a Brand Transplant

So far, you've learned how to raise your awareness, become more mindful, and observe the world around you, like Dave Daigle and his team did at the CDC. Then, you saw how your brain naturally finds patterns in what you've observed, like the mathematician and engineer Archimedes. In these first two steps of the Perpetual Innovation Process, your work was purely theoretical. You learned how to heighten your powers of observation and then how to distill them into patterns. With our third step—Relate—you'll move from theory to reality. The Relate step is how you take Observe and Distill and transition them into the real world.

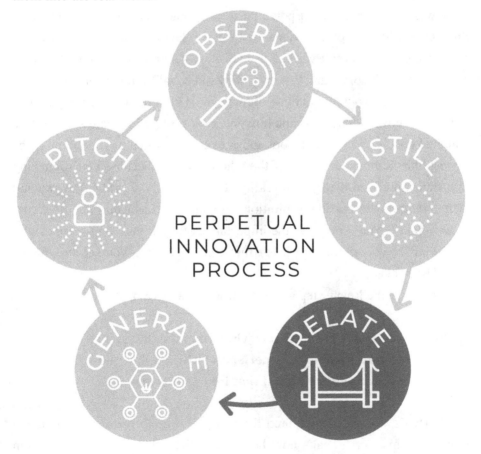

Relating is the process of seeing opportunities to tell a bigger story. When you relate bigger ideas and experiences to your work, you're looking at your organization from the outside in. Connecting the dots in this way means your harebrained ideas look less crazy and more credible. You've taken inspiration from something else that's already working and associated that with your own efforts.

Relating is an important step in the Perpetual Innovation Process, and one that can feel easy to rush through. I'll throw you a huge word of warning here: You *must* slow down and work through the Relate step rather than hopping right to Generate and slinging out ideas. If you don't, you'll end up in the copycat trap and miss the entire power of the Perpetual Innovation Process. Without understanding what it is about an idea or experience that relates to your work, you have a high potential to copy and paste, which is always a disaster. You'll try to push the idea forward, it'll fail miserably, and then you'll believe creativity doesn't work and innovation's a drag. It's too hard. It's for other people. It's something that only works in "cool" companies.

I understand your temptation—believe me, I do. I fell into this trap myself before I discovered its magic and how the most prolific innovators use it. I've watched people in my workshops gloss over it as a make-work step. To be honest, this is the hardest step of the whole process, because you're making that transition from theory into reality. This is how you bridge the gap and bring credibility to outside inspiration, so your final ideas don't come across as half-baked. You'll only see the importance of the Relate step in hindsight, after you've worked through it the first time. But once you see the magic, you'll be hooked.

I describe the Relate step as conducting a Brand Transplant.

**A Brand Transplant is when you take the essence
behind a great idea, experience, or brand that you see,
and you transplant that into your own work.**

In Ben's case, he transplanted the essence of a Hollywood movie experience into his work. That's how he realized that what made major motion pictures successful wasn't A-list actors and big budgets but rather being able to tell a story, create buzz, and build a following. It's that essence that he transplanted into his own work. In chapter 3, Tim Washer did the same thing with Ray Romano's stand-up act. He distilled his observations from the comedy club. When it came time to relate it to his own work, he transplanted the essence behind what he saw—building an intimate relationship in a short amount of time through humor. This is how he came up with the idea for his video that was phenomenally successful.

I'll give you a heads-up that as you work through this particular step, it's going to feel like there's an overlap between Relate and Generate (the next step). Resist the urge to look at your objective statement and try to solve the problem just yet. During the Relate step, we're still looking at your business as a whole; we're not yet looking at the problem from your Objective Statement.

Your mind has the ability to transfer the principles that are inherent in one thing to try to solve problems in another area. Creativity and innovation are about connecting the dots, but those dots have to have meaning. And, you need to be able to relate what you're experiencing in your everyday life to a bigger problem that you're dealing with. You've just distilled your observations into categories. Now, let's talk through exactly how to relate them to your world.

How to Relate: Four Steps

The Relate process (and the Brand Transplant) includes four steps:

1. **Compare.** Examine broader themes that you came up with in the Distill step. What similarities do you see? What about the differences? Go beyond the obvious, and don't be afraid to be silly with what you discover.

2. **Associate.** Determine which themes you notice have things in common with your brand. Be careful, though—it's not about coming up with ideas yet. We're still just connecting the dots and slowing down the idea-generation process. As you look for associations, you are looking at them between the patterns you identified in the Distill step and how any of them may relate to your brand.

3. **Prioritize.** If you've done your due diligence in coming up with more than 200 observations and 20 different patterns, then it's time to prioritize them. Not everything can be done at once, nor should it.

As you relate outside inspiration into your work, you'll need to rank which things matter the most and have the greatest meaning to your current situation.

4. **Attach.** Take the strongest correlations and use those to look at your brand with a new perspective. This seems like a little thing, but it's a subtle nuance that will be the spark for a massive amount of ideas in the Generate step.

You may be able to see relationships right away with some things, and others won't make any sense at all. You might find that you look at a couple of the categories you distilled, and together they spark something that relates to your situation. Again, you're not looking for any rhyme or reason with how things connect or what connects. There's no right or wrong. You're simply using your work from the Distill step as a way to organize what you observe and get it ready to relate it to your world.

How Might We...?

Dr. Min Basadur has spent more than four decades studying creative thinking, innovation, and problem-solving capabilites in companies. Through his work he's found one thing that radically stands out: The language that people use can stifle creativity instead of encouraging it. For example, if someone asks, "How should we solve this problem?" or "How can we solve this problem?" you've already begun to limit yourself. This is because words like *should* and *can* imply judgment. In the back of your mind, you'll be thinking, *Well...I'm not sure how we should solve it. In fact, I'm wondering if we should even try. We have so many priorities that maybe this isn't that big of a deal after all. Or, How can we solve it? Hmm...that I don't know. Because there's so many things that get shot down around here that honestly, even if we came up with a killer idea, I don't know if we could solve the problem because of all the internal politics.*

That's how he came up with the "How might we..." phrase that some of the most innovative companies in the world use. Companies like Google and design-thinking powerhouse IDEO. Min says that by substituting the word *might* for *can* or *should*, you're able to hold off judging the appropriateness or viability of what you're considering. This helps people open up to possibilites that they would otherwise discount as not feasible. And remember, you're not looking for any answers yet; that comes in the next step of the process, Generate.

Min learned this approach when he worked at Procter & Gamble in the 1970s. At the time, the company was in a heated battle against Colgate-Palmolive's popular new Irish Spring soap. This green-striped bar had P&G's marketers in a lather, trying to figure out how to beat the competition at the soap game. Instead of trying to copy the green bar, Min suggested looking at how to answer a bigger question. It wasn't about "How can we create a better green-striped bar," but rather "How might we create a more refreshing soap of our own?" By changing the nature of the question, Min redirected the situation and opened the creative floodgates of the marketing team. Out of this came the eventual idea of a coastal-blue-and-white-striped bar named Coast.

Here's how it works: Think of a simple question, such as getting your entire team to show up on time for an all-hands meeting every week. You know you're losing valuable time and spiking frustration levels with people dropping in at different times and some never showing at all. Ask yourself the problem-solving question in the three formats:

1. How should we get everyone to show up on time?
2. How can we get everyone to show up on time?
3. How might we get everyone to show up on time?

Lay this book down for a few minutes and pay attention to how your answers feel when responding to each of the question based on how they are worded. Like Min and his team, I believe you'll find broader answers when you ask the question in bigger terms. This is a key step in connecting the theoretical work in your previous steps to the real world in this one.

Putting It into Play

As you begin your Relate work, you will go back to your sticky notes (ideally using either a different color, or at least a different color marker). Look at each of the labels of your Distill categories. Then, as you compare, associate, prioritize, and attach, you'll find your brain working. You will now begin to associate your Distill topics to your own work with the phrase "How might we...?"

This step continues the build you've started with your sticky notes. Next to each of your Distill category headings, add a sticky note that has a single Relate question that starts with "How might we…?" Building on our coffee shop example, here's what my Perpetual Innovation process looks like at the Relate stage, starting with my Distill category of "Icky Things."

As you work through this process, you may wonder if you're finding the right questions to ask. Know this: There is no right or wrong in what you find. The purpose, again, is to develop your fluency in making the connections. For each of your Distill categories, see if you can create 10 to 15 connections through your Relate "How might we…" questions.

For my work, these are 15 Relate questions I came up with for my "Icky Things" category topic from my Distill step:

Icky Things
1. How might we make day-to-day tasks less disgusting?
2. How might we "clean up after ourselves" and keep from leaving a bad impression?

3. How might we discover the hidden ugly side effects of doing business with us?
4. How might we turn bad experiences into desirable ones?
5. How might we create an easier-to-use product?
6. How might we solve bigger problems for our customers?
7. How might we have a smaller environmental impact?
8. How might we recycle more?
9. How might we remove hurdles in doing business with us?
10. How might we simplify customer paperwork?
11. How might we keep from making people feel taken for granted?
12. How might we get customers to quit taking us for granted?
13. How might we quit wasting money on things that don't matter?
14. How might we cut down on employee absenteeism?
15. How might we lower employee burnout?

While my example is for one category, your exercise is to go back and do this for each of your Distill sticky notes. When you do this, you will set yourself up for a much easier experience as you move into the next step, Generate. At this point, you will have a sizeable number of ways to see how what you observed now relates to the work you do.

While you may struggle with the Relate step your first few times through, as you continue to practice it, you will become fluent and find yourself conducting Brand Transplants from even the most unrelated situations in which you find yourself. Before, you didn't have context for how any of this made sense, but now you should be seeing the start of connections. Now that you've done all this work, you'll move into the Generate step, where you'll dust off your objective, roll up your sleeves, and get to some really fun work.

CHAPTER 7

Step 4—Generate:
Becoming an Idea Factory

I t was a dreary, gray day in New York City. Kathy Button Bell sat in the back of a cab as it wound its way through the congested streets of SoHo. As the CMO of Emerson, she was in the midst of working her way through a new campaign during a rough time for business—the fallout of the economic crisis of 2009.

"Business was stressful," Kathy said. "I had been at an event with some customers. One of them turned to me and said he hoped our new ad campaign worked, because he just had to lay off 3,000 of his people. The pressure for industry to be successful while spending SG&A [selling, general, and administrative expenses] was huge."

Banks had reported losing more than $1 trillion since the beginning of the subprime mortgage crisis in 2007. In February 2009, Congress approved President Obama's economic stimulus package. But by March the stock market plummeted even more.

Kathy recalls sitting in her CEO's office as Maria Bartiromo, CNBC's "money honey," delivered bad headline after bad headline.

"She looked so tired and puffy...the wear and tear of what she reported was showing," Kathy explained. "Bad news on a daily basis and a stressed-out reporter. That was the environment in which we had to advertise."

It was a tough time for Emerson—a 125-year old, $24 billion global manufacturing company with 133,000 employees worldwide. Founded as a manufacturer of electric motors and fans, by 2012 it had grown into a Fortune 200 corporation that married technology and engineering for big industry, like oil and gas, chemical processing, commercial refrigeration, air-conditioning, telecom, industrial automation, and even home appliance and professional tools businesses. In 2002, Kathy launched the company's first corporate global advertising campaign with the tagline "Emerson. Consider It Solved," which gave it increased visibility and credibility in the marketplace.

The dilemma now facing Emerson was that despite its groundbreaking innovations, it wasn't perceived as either groundbreaking or particularly innovative as a company. Its competitors, such as GE, were seen as the *real* innovation leaders. It was an image Emerson needed to build if it was to have any chance of winning the highly competitive B2B global industrial space. The brand was being wildly outspent and out marketed by competitors when it should have been leaving them in the dust.

"We couldn't be seen as 'old reliable,'" Kathy emphasized. "So, we needed to shift perceptions in a big way. But we had a very small budget to make it happen. Our key competitors had budgets that dwarfed ours—in fact, in 2011 GE outspent us 20:1!" The company's focus and execution on new-to-the-world and new-to-the-business product innovation were the proof the world needed to give Emerson the innovation cred it deserved. But, the market environment for both customers and investors was difficult and both were buckling down and bracing for what they knew were more hard times to come.

Kathy's objective for the new campaign was clear: She needed new ideas to earn credit for Emerson's groundbreaking innovation so she could attract the attention of customers (the top 200 decision makers at Fortune 1000 companies), and investors (who managed the investment portfolios of huge corporations like Goldman Sachs) along with the analysts who served as their gatekeepers. All with a tiny budget and just months to make it happen.

She knew that the storyline of the campaign was spot on. She'd worked with Marcia Iacobucci, senior vice president and group creative director at DDB in Chicago, for over a decade. Together, they'd turned out work that had driven consolidation of the corporate brand and increased its credibility in the marketplace.

But this time, they had to make sure they showed up and sounded different than Emerson ever had before. "We needed to show up in unexpected ways but in expected places where our customers were used to seeing us," Kathy pointed out. She knew investors and analysts were technical and financial information junkies always looking for companies with groundbreaking innovation. However, she knew all their competitors were talking about innovation in the same way, and it all sounded alike. To highlight Emerson's innovation, the new campaign would need to feature success stories that showcased how its technology enabled its customers to do things that truly had never been done before. While everyone else talked innovation, Emerson would show it.

As the team worked on ideas for bringing the campaign to life, nothing fit the bill—it was all too conventionally corporate. Too rational and expected. Kathy needed fresher, unexpected ideas. And she needed them fast.

"People are joyful when the stock market is going up," she said. "We were trying to figure out a way to bring joy in a negative environment. To be the antithesis of the news."

And that's when she saw it.

Painted high up on the side of a brick building was an ad for Apple's new iPod Nano-chromatic. In it, there was a colorful, metallic rainbow of iPods, each dripping paint down toward the ground.

"It was Apple's ad that clicked in my mind with Emerson's point of view about hope," Kathy said. "We had a sense of urgency with our campaign, and Apple's colorful, bright, optimistic, and unexpected ad is what we needed to connect the dots."

She found a print version of the ad and sent it to Marcia. "Will this idea work for us?" she asked. "We were able to take Kathy's inspiration from the Apple ad—the feeling of brilliant colors conveying hope, optimism, and energy—and blend that with our new-to-the-business and new-to-the-world communication objective for the ad and come up with something dramatically new," Marcia explained.

The campaign featured a color palette that was bright, colorful, and filled with energy, which would show that Emerson was the optimistic face of global business and it would help customers innovate their way out of the tough economic climate. From using indie rock music and unexpected imagery on financial cable news, to minimal copy and an optimistic tone in major airports and the *Wall Street Journal*, everything was designed to feel very different from traditional corporate advertising to which their target audience was numb. In fact, Kathy and her team decided to avoid the overused word "innovation," altogether. Instead, they chose the bold declaration "It's Never Been Done Before" to show, rather than tell, Emerson's innovation chops.

Emerson "Never Been Done Before" posters, mobile screens, and airport take over photo.

The outcome was beyond anything Kathy and her team could have imagined. In *Fortune*'s World's Most Admired Companies survey, the definitive report card on corporate reputation at the time, which compared 687 companies in 57 industries and 30 countries, Emerson's electronics industry rank rose to number 4 from number 5 the previous year. In the same report, Emerson's industry rank for innovation witnessed the most dramatic change—up to number 4 from number 12 the previous year. For the first time ever, it made Thomson Reuters Top 100 Global Innovators list. A separate *Fortune* survey of C-level executives found that 88.9 percent were now more likely to consider buying Emerson products and services. The company's website traffic spiked by 366 percent, time on site jumped by 296 percent, and the number of people who revisited the site increased by 153 percent.

Emerson boldly struck up new conversations with its audiences, injecting consumer-like energy and emotion. They used a distinctive media mix to tell dramatic "never-been-done-before" stories. They dominated major airports with spectacular takeovers and animated LED. The team cascaded social marketing to connect customers and investors to the brand through rich media, synced units, in-banner videos, and mobile apps. They tapped into core financial communications and global business media to create a new perception about Emerson.

Investors now considered Emerson to be an innovation leader with near universal belief (97 percent based on an Emerson tracking study conducted with Harris Corporation) that it was a single marketplace leader in most of its industries. The next-best-performing Fortune 500 company measured received only 83 percent. Investor confidence in the brand's ability to deliver solutions rose with "offers credible solutions" showing a 26 percent rise and belief that it has a "clear vision for the future" up 32 percent. Emerson was now seen as *uniquely* able to deliver innovative solutions, with more than three times the confidence earned by a significant Fortune 50 peer.

In addition to all of these measures, the campaign improved confidence in Emerson's employees and restored pride in the brand.

What's the secret behind this kind of extraordinary success?

Marcia says repetition is the way to get better.

"You still have to go through the process every single time, but you just get faster at it," she explains. "We've done it so many times that it's now a habit, and we don't always think about it. A client can call me today and say they need a great idea by tomorrow, and I know our team can do it better than

90 percent of the rest of the world because we're practiced at coming up with successful, creative ideas on demand."

One Is the Loneliest Number

We're stuck in a vicious cycle. Bosses and clients need new ideas, so teams put their heads together. They work long hours, late nights, and weekends. They're looking for the next best thing that will catapult their company into the bull's-eye of our customer's attention and solve our biggest business problems.

The problem is that people are looking for the one great idea. The home run, the viral campaign, or the silver bullet. They're on the hunt for the single thing that will solve their problem. Your charge with the Generate step isn't to come up with the one idea that you think will address your objective, or even the right idea or the best idea. This is because if you usher that single source of brilliance into your boss's office, and they shoot that idea down, you're left with nothing. You're sent back to the drawing board to come up with the next one idea, you go back to your boss for approval, they shoot it down, and the cycle repeats itself.

This is why our careers teach us to avoid risk by avoiding new ideas. New ideas are scary, unpredictable, and a threat to the status quo. And, let's face it, given the choice between maintaining the status quo and having the courage to stick out your neck and try something new, you'll take the first route. You've seen all the work that goes into fearlessly proposing new ideas, and how quickly they get shot down.

The answer to this never-ending back and forth is to come up with as many ideas as you can, so if one gets shot down, you have more at the ready and don't have to keeping repeating the process to present more ideas. You have them in your back pocket, and you're ready on the spot.

The first three steps of the Perpetual Innovation Process are what make all the difference between conventional companies and innovative ones. Because it's these three steps that begin the idea generation process from a completely different perspective. Ideas generated from inspiration are powerful, which is why we need the first three steps of the Perpetual Innovation process. People struggle to come up with fresh ideas because they don't have a purpose or structure to them. We take care of that in the Generate step.

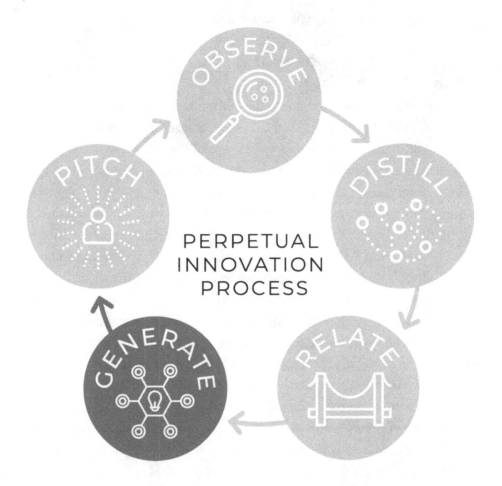

PERPETUAL
INNOVATION
PROCESS

The reason behind coming up with as many ideas as you possibly can is that in order to end up with a few ideas that are better ideas, you have to have to start with significantly more ideas. This is because plenty of them will be tossed to the side or die a painful death along the way. You may end up with some great ideas, but they'll never fly in your company's culture. Some could just be wrong timing. Others could be a lack of priority. Some could be they just won't execute well. And you know that there's plenty that will get crushed under corporate politics and narcissistic egos.

When you take all of this into consideration, you'll see that it's a numbers game. In order to have a few new, great, and reliable ideas standing at the end of the Generate step, you need to start out with a lot of ideas.

Now, it's time to roll up your sleeves and get started.

Generate on Purpose: Bringing Your Objective Back into the Picture

In the Generate step, we continue to move from the general to the specific.

Remember the Objective we came up with back in chapter 4? It's time to pull it off the shelf and revisit it. The part of the process that you'll walk through next is how to take all that you've observed, distilled, and related back to your brand and see how everything resonates with your original objective. Not everything will. But, if there's anything that even whiffs of a resemblance, you'll dig deeper into that and how it, specifically, relates to your objective. You'll need to work hard to resist the temptation to stop as soon as you find a couple of ideas that seem like good ones or even to slow down once you feel you've come up with *the* idea. Because, remember, a lot of what you come up with will remain behind on the cutting room floor for any number of reasons.

In the Relate step we looked at *How might we...* In the Generate step we ask, *what if we tried this? What if we combined two of these to come up with that?* All the lists of connections you've developed in the first three steps feed into this step to become your list of ideas.

At first, you may come up with enough good ideas that lead to your one great one, address your objective, and then stop. But you'll find that the more you go through this process, by the time you get here again, you'll feel turbocharged, excited, and ready to start reeling off things that pop into your head, seemingly out of nowhere. With practice, you'll find that ideas start coming to you as if out of nowhere—just like they do for Kathy Button Bell and Marcia Iacobucci.

In the Generate step, it's important not to impose limitations immediately. You want to pick out every connection you can. You literally want to come up with hundreds of ideas. At that point, you'll bring the constraints from your objective and use them as a filter for saying yes or no, or as a guide for the ones you choose to iterate. These will be the known limits within which you will need to function. That may cut your list of 200 ideas to 50. Then you'll think each of the 50 through and ask questions about priorities, timing, size, scope, resources, and so forth to narrow it down to your brilliant finalists. It's these lucky few that will move onto the next step of being pitched.

Let's revisit our objective statement structure:

1. **We need new ideas to…** What's the problem you're trying to solve? Your intention with this statement is to create clarity and focus.
2. **So we can…** Define the impact you want to have.
3. **With these constraints…** What are two to four limits you know this idea will need to live within?

For the sake of our Generate exercise, we'll continue with our objective from Chapter 4:

1. *We need new ideas…*for how we conduct global employee culture training.
2. *So we can…*improve employee engagement and retention.
3. *Constraints…*with the next 12 calendar months and for a budget of $500,000 or less.

Divide and Conquer

As you start this step, I'm going to have you break up your Generate work into two parts, leaving the refinement you'll do with your constraints until later. This is purposeful. You want to come up with ideas without judging whether they're workable or not. It's important to keep your mind free and open for as long as possible. As soon as you start to judge the viability of an idea, you kill your mojo and you get out of the flow. You're purely looking for fluency in coming up with ideas. We'll work your constraints in at the right moment. There's a time and a place for everything, as the saying goes, including your constraints.

You'll start by only using the first part of the objective statement:

1. We need new ideas…for how we conduct global employee culture training.
2. So we can…improve employee engagement and retention.

Go back to all of your Relate categories. Now, take the one that stands out the most—there doesn't have to be any reason for it standing out—and combine it with your objective statement.

How might we turn bad experiences into desirable ones?

As you combine it with your objective statement, you will create a question that looks like this:

> **How might we conduct global employee cultural training**
> **that turns bad experiences into delightful ones**
> **so we can improve employee engagement and retention?**

You've now created a question that combines the inspiration from observations at a coffee shop with a business objective you want to address. Your answers to this question will be your ideas for the Generate step.

Putting It into Play

It's time to go back to your sticky notes. If you think it's quicker or easier to write things down or have someone take notes on a laptop, it will create a kink in your process. By staying with the process of using a new color sticky note or pen for each stage and placing in where you can see it in relation to how you got there, it allows you to track your ideas backward. This helps you with context for the idea-generation exercise. Once you've gone through the Perpetual Innovation Process several times, you'll be able to jump back to parts in the middle, rework them, and come up with oodles of new ideas without having to start all over.

Plus, you'll use this flow from the Observe step into Generate for the Pitch step, so stay with this practice.

Now, start listing as many ideas that come to mind. As I worked through my Generate process, here are some of the ideas I came up with:

1. Have a feedback loop from more than one person or department so we understand what training matters most to people and what they don't like about what we're doing now.
2. Conduct an employee survey and ask their favorite ways to learn.
3. Gamify learning so employees can learn the lessons and the nuances in levels, win badges, and compete against others.
4. Have employees suggest ideas for an all-employee competition and have the top three winners be a part of its implementation.

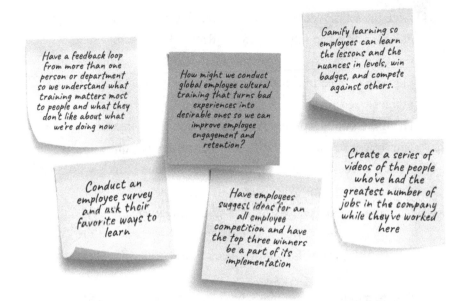

5. Create a series of videos of the people who've had the greatest number of jobs in the company while they're worked here.
6. Give the three people (non-executives) who've been at the company the longest a free trip to Bali.
7. Have every manager do a one-on-one with each of their direct reports four times a year to reinforce company culture so employees feel heard.
8. Give every employee an allowance of $25 per month to demonstrate the company culture outside of the company, e.g., give away a company T-shirt.
9. Give every employee one paid day off a month to volunteer for the non-profit of their choice that aligns with the value of the company's culture.
10. Hire comedians from Second City comedy troupe to create and deliver the training through a series of videos.
11. Close the entire company for one week every six months and have all employees go to an off-site resort for culture refresher and reinforcement.
12. Allow every employee to give out five on-the-spot rewards of $100 each when they see a coworker living out the cultural values.
13. Give every new employee a free trip to the company's headquarters in Paris.

14. Give the employee who does the best job of exhibiting the company's culture a free trip into space with Richard Branson.

15. Create a "Class of..." program so that people "graduate" and feel an ongoing connection as alumni to others who went through the training at the same time.

16. Have the youngest employees in the company train the most tenured employees so they see a different perspective to the culture.

17. Create a weekly sitcom that reinforces the company's values and culture and have employees star in it.

18. Create a weekly podcast with a *This American Life*—type theme that tells interesting stories internally to employees about the culture and gives examples of how employees live it and what it means to them and their work.

19. Create a daily cartoon that's both fun and educational to teach people about the company's culture.

What other ideas would you add?

As you may notice in my list, the first ideas that came to mind were quick but conventional and not especially creative. As I added to it, more creative ones popped into my head. You'll experience the same thing happening as you create your own list of ideas.

Spend at least 15 minutes coming up with as many ideas as you can think of. Once you feel that your well has run dry, go back to your Relate topics, choose another one, combine it with your objective statement, and go through the process again. If you're working by yourself, spend at least an hour on this step. If you're working as a team, you may need a couple of hours. This can be something you work on during one practice session, give yourself a break of a few hours or even a few days, and come back to it. What you'll find is that your mind keeps making connections, and when you revisit your work, you'll feel another sudden burst of ideas. You're done once you've worked through your list of Relate topics and in total have more than 200 ideas.

Now that you have your list, it's time to bring your constraints into the picture. One of the reasons executives think that creativity and innovation are "nice to have" rather than "must have" is because they don't see them as grounded in reality. Constraints are your reality check.

Believe it or not, the best ideas come when there are constraints. That's when you really start thinking in a unique fashion, because your brain sees the constraints as a puzzle. And your brain will continue to work on a puzzle until it solves it—it naturally likes to come to completion with things it works on. The constraints under which you generate ideas will be different for every situation, company, industry, period in time, or any other variable you can think of.

For our example, our constraints are that we have to implement our idea within the next 12 calendar months and for a budget of $500,000 or less. Assuming that we have a company with 10,000 employees worldwide, let's cross some of our ideas off the list that won't make this cut:

1. Have a feedback loop from more than one person or department so we understand what training matters most to people and what they don't like about what we're doing now.

2. Conduct an employee survey and ask their favorite ways to learn.

3. Gamify learning so employees can learn the lessons and the nuances in levels, win badges, and compete against others.

4. Have employees suggest ideas for an all-employee competition and have the top three winners be a part of its implementation.

5. Create a series of videos of the people who've had the most number of jobs in the company while they're worked there.

6. Give the 300 people (non-executives) who've been at the company the longest a free trip to Bali.

7. Have every manager do a one-on-one with each of their direct reports four times a year to reinforce company culture so employees feel heard.

8. Give every employee an allowance of $25 per month to demonstrate the company culture outside of the company, e.g., give away a company T-shirt.

9. Give every employee one paid day off a month to volunteer for the nonprofit of their choice that aligns with the value of the company's culture.
    *   *While it's beyond our budget, it can spin it into a marketing objective and reinforce the company's commitment to supporting local communities, so we're keeping it in.*

10. Hire comedians from Second City comedy troupe to create and deliver the training through a series of videos.

11. ~~Close the entire company for one week every six months and have all employees go to an off-site resort for culture refresher and reinforcement.~~

    • *Beyond our budget.*

12. Allow every employee to give out five on-the-sport rewards of $100 each when they see a coworker living out the cultural values

13. ~~Give every new employee a free trip to the company's headquarters in Paris.~~

    • *Beyond our budget.*

14. ~~Give the employee who does the best job of exhibiting the company's culture a free trip into space with Richard Branson.~~

    • *Beyond our budget.*

15. ~~Create a "Class of…" program so that people "graduate" from the program and feel an ongoing connection as alumni to others who went through the training at the same time.~~

    • *To succeed, this will need to go beyond 12 months.*

16. ~~Have the youngest employees in the company train the most tenured employees so they see a different perspective to the culture.~~

    • *To succeed, this will need to be an ongoing program that lasts more than 12 months.*

17. Create a weekly sitcom that reinforces the company's values and culture and have employees star in it.

18. Create a weekly podcast with a *This American Life*–type theme that tells interesting stories internally to employees about the culture and gives examples of how employees live it and what it means to them and their work.

19. Create a daily cartoon that's both fun and educational to teach people about the company's culture.

I've crossed off things that wouldn't work in the time and money constraints we have. While some could work if we adjusted the constraints, for the sake of this example I'm cutting them in this first round.

This is our first pass at filtering our list of ideas. Now, let's look at what's left after your first pass based on your obvious constraints and whittle things down a little further:

1. ~~Have a feedback loop from more than one person or department so we understand what training matters most to people and what they don't like about what we're doing now.~~
   - *This could be part of another project that relates to customer experience. On its own it won't affect company culture in the way we would like.*

2. ~~Conduct an employee survey and ask their favorite ways to learn.~~
   - *We already survey employees about so many topics that adding another one won't make this a good experience.*

3. Gamify learning so employees can learn the lessons and the nuances in levels, win badges and compete against others.
   - *This idea could be implemented within our constraints.*

4. ~~Have employees suggest ideas for an all-employee competition and have the top three winners be a part of its implementation.~~
   - *While a new idea, this one may be difficult depending on the willingness and availability of the employee to be a part of the implementation, plus their skill level.*

5. ~~Create a series of videos of the people who've had the greatest number of jobs in the company while they're worked there.~~
   - *Implementable, but not a solid enough idea on its own because the theme doesn't tie strong enough to turning bad experiences into good ones. It could potentially be combined with another idea down the road.*

6. ~~Give the 300 people (non-executives) who've been at the company the longest a free trip to Bali.~~
   - *This will cause hard feelings and disengagement between the people who get to go and those who don't.*

7. ~~Have every manager do a one-on-one with each of their direct report four times a year to reinforce company culture so employees feel heard.~~

- *Managers are already strapped for time and behind on doing regular performance reviews. This would add more of a burden than a benefit.*

8. Give every employee an allowance of $25 per month to demonstrate the company culture outside of the company, e.g., give away a company T-shirt.
    - *Implementable and it gives employees a tangible connection to the company.*

9. Hire comedians from Second City comedy troupe to create and deliver the training through a series of videos.
    - *Implementable, refreshing, and fun.*

10. ~~Have the youngest employees in the company train the most tenured employees so they see a different perspective to the culture.~~
    - *A different perspective, but the younger employees may not truly understand the culture. And their opinions on how it is expressed may not be relatable for older workers.*

11. Create a weekly sitcom that reinforces the company's values and culture and have employees star in it.
    - *Tapping into interns who would like to get experience with script writing and video production and editing could add a creative outside perspective to this option.*

12. Create a weekly podcast with a *This American Life*–type theme that tells interesting stories internally to employees about the culture and gives examples of how employees live it and what it means to them and their work.
    - *This idea is implementable within our time frame. The content that's created also has legs beyond the 12-month period. It could be especially interesting to have different employees change off over time as the host.*

13. Create a daily cartoon that's both fun and educational to teach people about the company's culture.
    - *This could be a fun way to get people engaged on a daily basis with what's going on in the company every day and make it fun.*

Could ask for an art intern to help with production to make it happen within budget.

Out of our original ideas from this one Relate category, we now have five solid ones that are new, great, and reliable while also fitting the constraints of our organization's culture:

1. Gamify learning so employees can learn the lessons and the nuances in levels, win badges, and compete against others.
2. Give every employee an allowance of $25 per month to demonstrate the company culture outside of the company, e.g., give away a company T-shirt.
3. Hire comedians from Second City comedy troupe to create and deliver the training through a series of videos.
4. Create a weekly sitcom that reinforces the company's values and culture and have employees star in it.
5. Create a weekly podcast with a *This American Life*–type theme that tells interesting stories internally to employees about the culture and gives examples of how employees live it and what it means to them and their work.
6. Create a daily cartoon that's both fun and educational to teach people about the company's culture.

How many ideas are enough? Quantity matters over quality when you're getting started. There's evidence that quality often doesn't max out until more than 200 ideas are on the table. In fact, in every field throughout history, the most innovative people produced a lot of output. Pablo Picasso was one of the most prolific artists of the 21st century. Isaac Asimov wrote more than 400 books. Aretha Franklin recorded 112 charted singles. In a mere five years, Thomas Edison filed for more than 100 patents for inventions that never went anywhere, but he needed to do that to get to the light bulb and the phonograph.

In our example, we've come up with five new, great, and reliable ideas just out of one Relate category. While that may not seem like a lot of ideas, think about this: You came up with five ideas from one Relate category. You have 8 to 10 Relate categories for every Distill topic. And you have around 20 different Distill topics. Simple math shows that by the time you work through all of the 200-plus observations you started with and get to the Generate step, you could potentially have 800 to 1,000 ideas!

Now you are equipped and ready to move to the last step of the Perpetual Innovation process: pitching the best of the best of your ideas. It's time to get support and start moving your ideas forward toward extraordinary outcomes.

CHAPTER 8

Step 5—Pitch:
Creating an Idea Journey

There's a scene in the first season of *Mad Men* in which creative director Don Draper pitches an ad to his clients at Kodak. The Sterling Cooper team invites the group into their sleek and elegant conference room to talk about the ideas that came out of their brainstorm.

The Kodak team admits that their product—the Wheel—isn't seen as exciting technology, even though the wheel actually is the original technology of humankind. That gives Don an opening. He says technology is a glittering lure, but the most important idea in advertising is the itch it creates around something "new." He goes on to talk about a deeper bond with the product—nostalgia.

Don shares the story of his early days in advertising when a seasoned copywriter taught him the value of nostalgia. "It's delicate...but potent," he says with a knowing wink.

The lights dim, everyone turns to the screen at the front of the room, and Don begins clicking through slides as images project on the screen. As he shows pictures of his children, his wife, and their life as a family, he talks about nostalgia as a twinge in your heart, far more powerful than memory alone. The Wheel is a device that goes backward and forward. "It takes us to a place where we ache to go again."

With that, he says to the Kodak team, the product isn't called the Wheel, it's called the Carousel. "It lets us travel the way a child travels, around and around and back home again to a place where we know we are loved." The slide of Don wearing a white tux and carrying his wife in her wedding dress is replaced by one that announces the Kodak Carousel slide tray.

Don Draper was a master at pitching. But let's face it: who has ever actually had a pitch that comes out as eloquent and captivating as that? None of us. Although this is how pitches were actually designed to work, that's not how they turn out in the real world.

A Pitch Is More than a Good Idea

Every great idea needs support to go somewhere. Great pitches paint a picture and connect the dots between a new idea and the business needs of a brand. Most people pitch their great idea but don't give people the context behind it. If your audience doesn't get behind it, your idea will never go anywhere—it doesn't matter how great it is. Truth be told, you'll hear "No!" over and over again. That's why you get frustrated and end up falling back on the same old boring work that you've always done. A big way out of that hole of despair and frustration is by getting better—a lot better—at your pitch.

We're now at the point in the Perpetual Innovation Process where you'll learn how to tell a story that brings your audience along for the journey. At its very root, that's exactly what a pitch is.

A Pitch is the journey of an idea told in the form of a story.

You've heard the cliché that great ideas speak for themselves. Actually, that couldn't be further from the truth. In fact, bad pitches kill great ideas. If you don't know how to tell the story of your ideas in a way that keeps people's attention and makes it sound new, great, and reliable, you'll always struggle to

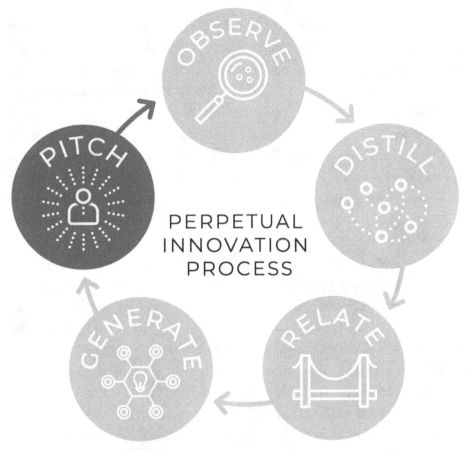

get backing for them. A pitch is more than "Hey, I have a great idea—wanna hear it?" In fact, if that's been your practice, then you've been hurting your chances of getting your ideas adopted.

The Gladiator Effect

Andrew Davis could come up with a million great ideas. But he knew he needed more than that to be successful in Hollywood.

With a degree in film and television, Andrew produced shows for NBC's *Today* show, worked for the Muppets, and wrote for Charles Kuralt. Not only did he regularly pitch ideas and cross his fingers that someone would give him the thumbs-up, but he spent plenty of time on the other side of the desk hearing people present to him as a producer. He experienced firsthand the difference between bad pitches and successful ones.

"The best pitches are when you paint a vivid enough picture in a short amount of time for the people you're pitching to," Andrew explains, "but leave enough unsaid that they can imagine it the way they want to imagine it."

He points out that too many people try to anticipate every possible question and address it up front. Doing this makes you inflexible with people's input. When they ask questions or give you feedback, you feel they're questioning the idea, and you naturally defend it, rather than listen for thoughts that can make it better. But when you paint just enough of the picture for people to see the idea in a way that makes sense for them, they ask questions to fill in the blanks.

"When they start asking questions," Andrew says, "then you know they're engaged. That's when you can finish creating the rest of the idea together." When others become a part of developing your idea, they'll support it.

Not every idea turns into a workable one. It's a gamble, for sure. And just like playing the slots or blackjack, it's a numbers game. When that happened in TV, Andrew and the idea people leaned on a tool called the pitch book—a book that's filled with ideas. Some are fully flushed out, and others are nothing more than a log line—a one-sentence explanation of a show.

"A show book is a book filled with ideas you've already come up with for shows," Andrew explained. "You only have a small window of time with a producer. If you get a no on your first idea, you still have a portfolio of ideas to work through. You go through the show book one concept after another because you have to go through a lot of ideas to get to the best ones. In TV, you have to have a lot of ideas ready to go." This process, he points out, shows the catcher—the person to whom you're pitching, who's deciding whether or not they'll catch your idea—that you're capable of coming up with a lot of great ideas and have them at the ready. The catcher gives the pitcher feedback one by one, and they roll through the list of ideas together.

This notion of being open to a lot of ideas in TV transfers into success in other situations.

"The most innovative corporate environments are the ones in which top management welcomes an idea, no matter how bad it is," Andrew points out. "More ideas mean better ideas."

One of the reasons is that we've been conditioned by the Gladiator Effect.

In ancient Rome, gladiators were swordsmen who entertained crowds by fighting other gladiators in large arenas. The destiny of the gladiators was determined by the crowds who watched, and they signaled the fate of the battle with a thumbs-up or a thumbs-down. The outcome was black and white.

The same thing happens in business today with new ideas. People pitch a single new idea, and they get a thumbs-up or a thumbs-down. The idea either lives or dies—just like the gladiators. This is what feeds into the head-butting between bosses and teams. Bosses and clients demand new, great, and reliable ideas on a consistent basis. But when teams try to produce them, nothing survives. They're sent back to the drawing board and expected to come up with the next one. It's thrust into battle against the boss or client, and the team holds their breath waiting to see if it gets a thumbs-up or a thumbs-down.

When you pitch a new idea and it doesn't survive the Gladiator Effect, it does more than squash your new idea. Little by little, it kills your courage. And no one can become a Perpetual Innovator without courage.

Are we locked in a status quo stalemate?

Luckily, no.

You change this dynamic by breaking the Generate and Pitch cycle.

When you need new ideas for something—a better customer experience, a strategic plan, a campaign—what do you do? You gather everyone into a conference room and start throwing out ideas. You brainstorm and fill whiteboards and walls with your best ideas. Because, you say, there's no such thing as a bad idea.

But people come to the table with horrible pitches. They're generic rather than personalized. They're dry and put the audience to sleep. There's no structure, and they haven't done their homework about the true problem that needs to be solved. This is because they don't have a process that allows them to draw on a portfolio of experiences that inspires them, or they don't know how to relate those ideas back to their own brand. They pitch these "great" ideas, and their boss, coworker, or client doesn't have any context for where the idea came from or how it relates to the work that you do. And when that happens? It triggers Brand Detachment Disorder for the catcher, and they tell you things like:

We don't sell those kinds of products.
Our customers have a different process for making decisions.
We tried that once, and it didn't work.
We don't have it in the budget.
That's ridiculous.
Or the biggest idea killer of all:
That's not how we do things around here.

Good Ideas Don't Speak for Themselves

Up until now, you've been working on coming up with your best-of-the-best ideas.

Coming up with great ideas is its own challenge, but convincing others to give them the green light is another ball of wax altogether. It doesn't matter if you're pitching a new recruitment process, marketing campaign, software feature, accounting protocol, organizational change, or business plan, the qualities of a successful pitch are largely the same. And it starts with knowing how to set the stage, so you lay the groundwork for a successful pitch.

Prep Step 1: Know Your Audience (the "Catchers" of Your Idea)

Before you start your pitch, you have to make sure you know your audience, what matters to them, and how your pitch fits into their world. Is it your boss? Your team? A client? An investor? You need to clearly understand who they are, what you know about them, and where you need to do your homework. These are the things that will help you add nuance to your story based on who you're pitching to. The question you'll constantly ask yourself as you pick and choose the tidbits to include is, *what matters most to this person?* You need to be ready to address the idiosyncracies of an investor versus those of your team. The questions you'll need to answer include:

1. What's an overview of their day? And how does the time that you'll ask to pitch your idea fit into that? If they're a morning person, don't wait until late afternoon to get together. And if they're a night owl who needs time for their brain to warm up, don't schedule an early-morning meeting.

2. How does this idea fit into their world? For example, if they're a technical person, do you need their support so they can give you the experitise of their team? Or, if it's someone in fiance and they need to approve the budget, what's the filter through which they'll be looking at your idea?

3. WIIFT? *What's in it for them?* is a big one. While you need to connect your idea to a business objective, you also need to understand what motivates them. Are they trying to improve their chances for a promotion? If so, make sure to include a bent that shows how the project will make them look good. Are they lookig to make their department more productive so they can work fewer nights and weekends? Or maybe it's your client who really wants to change the perception of their organization, but they're not sure they're the ones who should make the first move. All of these details make a difference in what details you hang on the strucutre of your pitch.

Prep Step 2: Develop Multiple Versions

Now that you have a sense of who you'll pitch to, you need to create multiple versions of different lengths. You may have a meeting set up in which you'll give your boss a fancy presentation—then she sees you in the hallway and cancels. You'll have a small window to give her a quick rundown, and you need to be ready. Opportunities often come up when you least expect them, and you have to be ready—in the lunchroom, the hallway, team meetings, suggestion boxes, and even someone you meet in a shared cab. Make sure your story is ready to go.

As you put the pieces together, always formulate your pitch into three levels of depth:

*   30 seconds
*   90 seconds
*   5+ minutes

The 30-Second Version

Also known as the elevator pitch, this is the most concise version of your idea. You'll need to refine and practice and refine and practice again until you can make it impactful and interesting in a short amount of time. If you say your idea is too complex to be able to whittle it down to 30 seconds, then you haven't clearly mapped out your pitch from inspiration to idea. An unfocused process leads to an unfocused pitch.

This is the version you'll give to someone on the run or quickly in an off-the-cuff situation. Someone may introduce you and say you have a great idea on which you're working, or you find a potential investor at a cocktail party. It's short, deliciously interesting, and to the point. Your intention with this version is to get them to say, "Tell me more," so you can either move into your 90-second pitch right away or schedule time for a 5-minute or more conversation.

The 90-Second Version

This version will naturally grow out of your 30-second version. With this one, there's more time to talk about what you covered in 30 seconds or expand a little bit on what you think is the most important part of your pitch. Poke at the pain you know they're dealing with on a personal level. Sure, this idea may save a boatload of money, but what if it's also just the thing that will help them get the employee base to quit complaining and finally take action? What if it meant they could walk down the hall and not have 13 employees bend their ear with criticism? You also have a little elbow room to show how you've already thought through some of the obstacles. This is your chance to drill down into the next level of detail, adding in just enough interesting nuggets so your catcher gets a clearer picture of your idea, gets a deeper and more nuanced understanding of what you're proposing, and sees what's in it for them.

This version gives you a little more time. Perhaps you run into your client at lunch and you need to give them enough details so they'll make room for you on their calendar this week. Or maybe you want to grab your boss's attention so your idea can get the go-ahead and become a part of her presentation to the executive team on Monday. Your motivation with this version is to get to the 5-minute pitch.

5-Minute+ Version

This longer version could be five minutes, or it could be an hour. You may find that people start getting engaged, and ask you questions along the way, and the conversation goes much longer than five minutes. That's OK. It's a great sign that you've set the stage and engaged people on a journey that matters to them and they see themselves in the story. And, as Andrew Davis points out, they're helping you fill in the details with how they imagine the outcome. As long as you have their time and attention, take advantage of it!

You'll want to prepare ahead of time for this longer pitch. Maybe you'll put together a handout or a visual presentation. Make sure that whatever you do with either, you keep it interesting, don't get bogged down in details and numbers, but do be prepared to answer a wider range of questions than your shorter pitches.

The difference between all of these is that they move your catcher from interest to engagement to action. Few people will say yes to a 30-second pitch, but it can be enough that they'll ask for more. In 90 seconds, you have enough time to whet their appetite and hit their big pain points or show they have a lot to gain from your idea. Your five-minute plus meeting is when you lay it all out on the line. Regardless, they all need structure and an interesting storyline. The Perpetual Innovation process gives you exactly that.

Prep Step 3: Test Your Pitch

The longer you spend with an idea, the more vulnerable you become to blind spots and your own ego. Push yourself away from your desk and go find smart people to give you feedback. For example, as I worked through the Perpetual Innovation Process in this book, I regularly gathered feedback from my husband, Ron, and our next-door neighbor Jeremy. Then I bubbled things up to peers, clients, and people already knee-deep in innovation. I worked through pitch after pitch until I knew I'd nailed the process. If my pitches made it through this tight-knit group I trusted to give honest feedback, I was onto something. They were all savvy businesspeople who helped me see glaring gaps and then work through how to fix them. I didn't always get the feedback I wanted or liked, but they helped me sharpen my idea and how I told the story.

Only when I'd done that did I start testing it on people I identified in the first prep step as my audience.

When you look for people to give you feedback on your idea, seek out those you know will give you candid advice. You'll want folks who will talk things through in detail and help you with nuances. Just swapping out one word for another can take your pitch from fine to fabulous. I looked for people with experience in different areas of the business, who had worked with a range of people from execs to front-line employees. Those who had responsibility for outcomes, including profit and loss, and had executed ideas at scale. I also looked for people who had to pitch ideas over and over again as a part of their work. There's nothing like feedback from people who've done what you're wanting to do to help you improve your performance.

The Amazon fallacy says that friends and family are the worst people to test something on. But I used them for a reason—Ron and Jeremy worked in different areas of business than me. They were also excellent at working with and through processes that had to be sustainable and scale. They were honest to a fault, but they also knew how to dig into the minutiae of my pitch, talk it through with me, and help me work out all of the kinks. You need someone who has a vested interest in your work, and this dynamic duo was the first threshold for me. If it passed their scrutiny, then I knew it was ready to go to the next level.

Each time you test your pitch, you'll develop a list of questions that you'll be sure people will ask. Write them down and be prepared to answer them, in case anyone asks. How will you know what questions to prep for? Unfortunately, the only way to know is to practice your pitch with a diverse group of people.

But remember what Andrew Davis said earlier in this chapter: Don't try to answer everyone's questions up front with your pitch. Leave room for them to fill in the holes with their imagination. You want to paint just enough of a picture that people can see themselves in it but leave it vague enough that they have room to fill in the details. It's these details that build an emotional triangle between them, your idea, and you.

Prep Step 4: Practice Your Pitch

If you talk to someone who's an athlete, artist, or musician, they understand practice. Someone who's a veteran shows up very differently from a beginner. People who practice what they do are more competent, which expresses itself as greater confidence. And confidence is magnetic. There's a loop between competence and confidence. The more you do something, the more competent you become, which gives you confidence. And the more confident you are about your abilities, the more likely you are to continue to hone them, so you'll get better, or more competent. When your competence rises, so does your confidence.

The more you practice your pitch, the more focused you'll become. You won't be worried about making mistakes, forgetting one part, or talking too much during another. By the time you open your mouth to say the words, it will feel that they tumble out without you needing to give them a thought. The pitch has become a habit. You'll learn to be calm and confident and will actually have room to have fun with it. Then, sit back and listen to feedback. Like any kind of public speaking situation, the more often you do it, the more comfortable you will become.

By this point you've already come up with a list of potential questions or reasons people may say no. You'll need those. But also prepare for getting your dream response. If your catcher gives you the go-ahead and then asks what you need to get started, make sure you're prepared with that answer as well. Do you need them to help grease the organizational wheels? Do they need to sign a form? Dedicate a specific team? Know the first few steps you'll want to take and what they look like so there's no chance of them saying, "Think about it and get back to me." That, in and of itself, could be a reason your fabulous idea gets killed down the road. Capture enthusiasm and support the moment you receive it.

Putting It into Play

For the pitch, you'll bring people along on an idea journey from your initial inspiration through the execution. You'll trigger anticipation by showing people what's possible and getting them excited about the future.

You'll use the same Perpetual Innovation Process you just used to come up with new ideas, showing people how you've connected the dots along the way. This brings a fresh perspective—but with context—into your work, tells the story of a new idea, and, most importantly, inspires your audience to feel vested in your success.

When people pitch, they miss two vital parts of the Perpetual Innovation Process, and what they end up doing is asking for permission to copy and paste ideas from someone else. I've even had heads of innovation tell me this is one of their biggest challenges with their team: People don't know how to dig into their inspiration and tell the story of how it connects to what matters to their company. People observe something in the world around them, they use that as their own idea (so, not a lot of actual work goes into generating an idea), and then they pitch that as a new concept. They skip the parts about distilling the meaning behind what they observed and doing a Brand Transplant that relates it back into their own work.

For comparison, here's how people pitch ideas today:

> Comedians are so funny! **(Observe)** We should hire comedians to make videos for our employee orientation sessions. **(Generate)** Let's differentiate ourselves by hiring comedians to make videos about our company culture! **(Pitch)**

This idea sounds crazy because your boss doesn't have context for why this matters or the value it can deliver. And to be honest, if you're the one pitching this idea, you don't truly understand how to take the essence behind the idea of using comedians and make it apply in the environment of your own company. Even if you got the green light, your idea would fail because you don't understand the underlying principles that would make it successful.

Now, compare that with how you can deliver a solid pitch by using the Perpetual Innovation Process. You'll connect the dots so everything from your inspiration to your idea feels natural for your audience:

> I was thinking about new ways that we could conduct our employee culture training. **(Objective part 1)**

And I was in a coffee shop the other day, and I started looking around at all the different people and sensations that happen when you spend time there. I noticed a guy chewing his nails, the smell of a poopy baby diaper, and trash on the floor. **(Observe)** Usually, we only think of the great smells and the relaxing feeling we have when we're in a coffee shop. But when you spend time in one, and pay attention to all the little details, the experience can be very different. When you stop and look around, there are a lot of icky things that people encounter in a situation that should be fun and relaxing! **(Distill)**

Then I began to wonder, how might we be doing icky things that we don't think about when we conduct global employee culture training? What are we not seeing? For example, are we doing things that make people feel bad about the mistakes they make? Are we making them feel like they can't be themselves at the office? Here's why this idea in particular jumped out at me: Who's really good about pointing out things that people don't see? Comedians! And, they do it in a way that makes people laugh and put down their emotional walls. **(Relate)**

That's what led me to an idea…What if we invested $500,000 over the next 12 calendar months and hired comedians from Second City to help us with culture training? They're experts at getting people's attention and keeping it in even the toughest situations. They can teach us how to avoid the common pitfalls that bore people to death in situations like this, and we can take what we learn and apply it in other areas of training. We'll learn how to make people engage through humor, how to open the lines of communication, and how to get people excited about something that right now, to be honest, they dread. **(Generate with constraints)** By doing this, I think we'll be able to improve employee engagement and retention. **(Objective part 2)**

If you were to outline your 30-second, 90-second, and 5-minute pitches, following are outlines you can use. As you'll see, each one builds on the previous version.

The 30-second pitch

- **Objective part 1.** Get right to the point. What's the outcome you believe you can deliver because of your new idea? Show right away the impact you believe you can have, and your catcher will be willing to hear the next sentence.

- **Observe.** It's important to show where the inspiration for your idea came from, but don't belabor it. If you do, you'll lose their attention fast.

- **Distill.** Remember, people's brains are looking for patterns. Moving into the bigger picture that you've uncovered because of what you discovered helps your catcher quickly get context. This keeps their brain engaged, and you move to the next step.

- **Relate.** Now is when the power really comes into play. Make sure your Brand Transplant is crystal clear. Remove any chance of them having to work to connect the dots in this step. This is when your idea transitions from theory to reality.

- **Generate with constraints.** You want to share enough of your idea to whet their appetite. By adding in the constraints, you've shown that it's not something that's pie in the sky. Even though you're just giving them the skinny, you're showing that you're being realistic about the hurdles you need to maneuver.

- **Objective part 2.** Ending with the second part of the objective ties your idea back into the real world. It solidifies it in their world and reinforces that the reason you're doing this is to have an impact on the business. Without that, the wheels will fall off the bus pretty quickly.

The 90-second pitch

- **Objective part 1.** You have a little more time to expand on the problem that you see, but you still don't want to overdo it. Your purpose of starting out with the first part of the objective is to bring your catcher into the same story that you're in, so you go forward in the conversation together. Your purpose with this statement is to pull people forward.

- **Observe.** Give a few more details in this round and make them interesting. Now you have an opportunity to paint a picture they can step into sooner.

- **Distill.** Dive a little deeper into the context. The more you can set the stage here, the easier it will be for them to make the leap in the next step.

- **Relate.** Slow down as you get to this step, and make sure that you have their full attention. Do this step right, and you'll make sure they see your idea as a novel one, rather than a cut-and-paste attempt at what someone else has already done.

- **Generate with constraints.** As you transition into your idea, you'll have time to give a few more details. You know you're on the right track when they stop anything they're doing and give you their full attention. Bring up the constraints, and if you've hit the right note with your pitch, they'll say things like, "Don't worry about that now..." That means they're fully into your idea, and they're willing to help work around the obstacles to see it through.

- **Objective part 2.** Every pitch needs to end with power. Tying your idea back to the beginning by explaining the outcomes you expect helps them imagine success on the other side. The more you can get them to see the new reality, the more they're minimizing the obstacles between where you are now, and where you want to take them.

The 5-minute+ pitch

- **Objective part 1.** For this version, spend time setting the stage for the problem you're wanting to solve. You and your catcher have a lot on your plate. Now that you have the time together, use it to make sure that you're both on the same page and pointed in the same direction. They may be looking at the same situation and think everything's hunky-dory. But what happens if no action is taken? A situation may not seem like that big of a problem until someone points out how big it can grow—and how fast—if nothing is done. It's always better to prevent a problem than to have to fix one. Or, how will your catcher feel down the road when they didn't take advantage of an opportunity when it was right under their nose? When opportunities come up, timing is everything.

- **Observe.** Take time to paint a vivid picture. Make sure to include details about all the things you took in—the sights, sounds, smells, taste, and things you touched. Make your description vivid so it feels as if your catcher were there themselves. You can cover a variety of details you observed but focus on the ones that lead to your Distill topic.

- **Distill.** Now you have an opportunity to go beyond just explaining how all of your Observe dots connect. As you talk through the pattern(s) you notice, share some insights. Are these things that you're seeing as trends in general? Did this experience bring something to your attention that you weren't able to put your finger on previously? Your brain makes patterns for a reason. Explain the significance of the ones you found.

- **Relate.** Again, make sure you don't rush through this step of your pitch. Remember how this was the toughest one as you went through the Perpetual Innovation Process? It's just as important that you're clear about how what you came up with during the Distill step matters to the work you, your department, or your company is doing. This is the key to making sure your idea doesn't come across as a copy and paste, but rather a truly original idea.

- **Generate with constraints.** Now you're getting into the meat of your pitch. If you're talking story arcs, this is the climax. You've laid the groundwork that shows how you got to today's idea, and now you must spend enough time to do it justice. Again, you're painting enough of the picture so your catcher can see themself in it, but you're keeping it streamlined enough that they'll help you fill in the details. This gives them a vested interest in the idea. By giving them space to fill in the details as they see it, you allow them to communicate what matters most to them. This helps you build their interest and also their likelihood of approving whatever you're asking for. Let the good idea sink in and let them wallow in it before you bring up the constraints. The more attractive you make your pitch, the easier it will be to get their help overcoming the roadblocks.

- **Objective part 2.** You need to end with strength and confidence. Wrapping up with the outcome you expect is powerful because you're painting the picture of the benefits they will experience once they move forward with this idea. Everyone wants to know what's on the other side. This is your chance to spell it out. Like every other step in this longer version of your pitch, it's about painting a picture. But this one in particular is about creating the dream of a better tomorrow because of your idea.

Now it's your turn. Use the space below to write out your pitch:

Objective Part 1

_____

_____

Observe

_____

_____

_____

_____

_____

Distill

_____

_____

_____

_____

_____

Relate

_____

_____

_____

_____

_____

Generate with Constraints

_____

_____

_____

_____

_____

Objective Part 2

_____

_____

_____

_____

_____

When you tell the journey of your idea through a process that people can follow, you reduce the perceived risk of trying something new. It also builds your courage and confidence so you're more willing and likely to do it again and again.

Giving and Receiving Feedback

When people bring new ideas to the table, there's a lot of responsibility.

Teams pitching ideas need to deliver a credible pitch that brings their audience—bosses, supervisors, peers, clients, etc.—along for the ride. Using the same Perpetual Innovation process to tell the story of your idea helps you do exactly that.

But the people hearing the pitch *also* have a great deal of responsibility. There's much more to giving feedback than just a thumbs-up or thumbs-down. Getting better ideas means giving better feedback.

Everyone who's put in the time and effort and backed it with courage to present a new idea deserves specific, helpful feedback.

- **Bosses:** It's your job to boost the courage of your team and give them the kind of feedback that refines ideas.
- **Individuals and teams:** You need to ask for feedback in a way that gives you the kind of direction that lets you nurture and refine your ideas.

To build a team of Perpetual Innovators, you need to create an environment that positions feedback in steps using two phrases.

The first phrase is *What I like...* This takes the focus off the person who brought the idea to the table and puts it on the idea itself. It begins to bring objectivity into the equation. It gives people validation that they did the right thing. When you start with the positive side of feedback, that leads to excitement. If someone has taken the initiative to stand before you and share their idea, start with at least that. Think it through and look for other things you like, even if they are small.

But let's face it. Few ideas are great ideas from the get-go. That's why we have to make sure that we give and get feedback to make first ideas better ideas.

The second phrase is *What I wish...* This changes the dynamic of feedback, removes the emotional negativity, and makes it feel less critical. This response gives individuals and teams guidance and lets them know where to spend their time. This is when you give direction about the areas that you'd like to see refined. When this person shows up at your door with a revised pitch, what do you want to make sure they have in it? Bosses find that they're able to give direction and point people toward a bigger goal or a larger picture. Both feel vested in the idea and neither end up defensive.

New, Great, and Reliable Ideas Require Perpetual Innovators

People take pitching for granted. But there's a lot of skill that goes into creating and delivering a powerful pitch that helps people see themselves in your picture and then inspires them to take action. Pitching is the easiest part of the Perpetual Innovation Process to overlook. It's important to focus on this step as much as the others, rather than just dabbling in it, because this is how you bring your idea all the way home with a strong finish. It's the capstone of your work, rather than an afterthought.

Are you excited? I hope so! Because, let's face it, none of us go into the line of work we're in to do status quo work. It doesn't matter how long you've been working, what industry you're in, or what rank you have in the company, anyone can be excited and successful about bringing new ideas to the table. When you follow the Perpetual Innovation Process to develop and pitch your ideas, you'll feel more competent, confident, and excited about the work you do.

But I have to point out that just following this process as a single innovator (even a Perpetual Innovator) won't make your entire company more innovative. You are one piece—an important one—in helping your team and your entire company think differently. But you still need an ecosystem that encourages people to practice creativity, take risks, and be willing to compete on a broader scale.

Now, let's talk about how to do this across your entire organization.

PART 2
The Practice

I used to love to play with rubber bands when I was a kid. I'd weave them into infinity rings on my fingers. I'd shoot them across the classroom. Given a packet I'd make a sizeable ball and play catch with it. If I could find a big one, I'd put it around my head and pull my nose back flat so I looked like a pig.

That's the beauty of rubber bands. The more you use them, the more pliable they become. And the more uses you find for them. Rubber bands are loaded with potential energy, and they stretch when they're put to good use.

But have you ever opened a drawer and pulled out a rubber band you haven't used in a while? It's brittle, and the rubber has a weird, white flaky texture to it. Try to stretch it just a bit, and it immediately snaps on you. There's no elasticity left, and it's lost all of its potential energy.

The same holds true with people.

You now know what innovation is and why it's so important. You have a process for consistently coming up with new, great, and reliable ideas. And yet, I guarantee you'll still struggle to get it right, primarily because your idea of innovation misses the people piece. It's easy to say that your company isn't innovative because your employees don't come to the table with any worthwhile ideas. Or maybe they aren't stepping forward at all. But in all honesty, it's the culture of your organization that doesn't allow people to act in a way that's natural to them.

> Corporate culture is a fundamental roadblock or gas pedal for innovation.

Corporate culture is a fundamental roadblock or gas pedal for innovation. It defines what your business is, why it does what it does, and confesses the unspoken story behind the brand. Culture directs what people think and how they work. It creates tangible and invisible restrictions, establishes risk tolerances, and sets standards about what people think and how they behave. This inherent code lets people know when they've gone too far and that they need to step back in line. It communicates an unspoken pecking order.

Companies tout innovation as a core value and cultural norm, but in the next breath home in on efficiency. The innovation process is one of the most—if not *the* most—inefficient things in which a company can invest. The system of coming up with ideas that have potential, vetting them, giving them a try, and seeing what works is, by its very nature, inefficient. Yet, organizations treat innovation as if you can make it a foolproof process. Executives insist that employees bring research and data to the table to de-risk new ideas. They want projections that squeeze out any chance of failure. By stripping out all the liability, leaders also remove potential energy. It's like putting your employees in a drawer, similar to rubber bands, and then expecting them to be massively innovative on a moment's notice without letting them practice the skills that will let them perform. They no longer have the capacity to stretch like they need to at a moment's notice.

From the time you're five until you're 65, society and then corporate culture teach innovation out of you. When you transition from university to the working world, you have dreams of big ideas. But year after year, you're taught to keep your head down and don't make waves. Instead of consistently nurturing and testing your innovative nature, it's all put in a drawer and left to atrophy. Then one day there's a new mandate to "be more innovative." And without clarity about what innovation even is, what it looks like, or how to do it, management expects you to immediately change your attitudes and behavior. Without practice and nurturing, just like an old rubber band, you'll snap under pressure. You're being asked to perform in a way that you're not skilled or practiced doing.

Consider this about a performance mentality: The average tennis match lasts two hours. Superstar Serena Williams trains to be able to last on the court for four hours or more. During peak training season, Olympic champion Michael Phelps swam a minimum of 80,000 meters a week—nearly 50 miles—to train for the Olympics. Not everyone wants to, or will, become that level of athlete. But what Serena and Michael understand is that being good at something requires consistent practice. If you don't build your muscle strength in little ways every day, you'll never be able to perform when the time comes, whether you're an athlete or an innovator. Especially on a moment's notice—which regularly happens in the corporate world. When you're asked to do more than you're prepared for in sports, you end up with injuries, a bad attitude, and quitters. In the same way, people in organizations give up when you expect too much of them and they've been given no time, support, or guidance on how to prepare. They know failure is inevitable, so why try?

Managers teach employees short-term thinking: Make sure we hit sales this month. Don't invest long-term because shareholders care about this year's dividend. Don't stick your neck out, or you can kiss that promotion goodbye. If you want to make improvements, make sure they don't involve risk.

In these situations, even incremental improvements are met with hurdle after hurdle. It's incredibly hard to change people's attitudes, mindsets, and behaviors. That's why companies that need innovation the most have cultures that are the least likely to change. When you try to keep operations fixed, to keep things efficient and hold on to your competitive edge, you'll find your culture resistant or, even worse, toxic when it comes to welcoming change—the kind of change you need to embrace innovation. It's the "If it ain't broke, don't fix it" mentality followed by the "We've always done it this way" excuse.

A culture that supports innovation encourages people to open up to uncertainty and take on reasonable risk when you're going after a bigger, predefined objective. It's a culture based on experimenting and discovery, because leaders understand that to have better ideas, you have to start with more ideas. Innovative cultures have porous boundaries. People and ideas constantly flow in and out of groups. When failure happens, rather than sweep it under the rug, people honestly try to learn from it. They know it's ridiculous to think you can have success without some level of inevitable failure.

Highly original, innovative cultures boldly defend innovation as a habit rather than happenstance. They don't treat it as an occasional, sporadic effort. These environments welcome different points of view and perspectives and look at connecting the dots between wildly diverse ideas. It's rare to hear someone in a perpetually innovative organization say, "We've never done it that way," as a preventative measure to shut down ideas. Instead, they're excited about new challenges and seeing if they're worth pursuing.

What do people, teams, and companies look like who think this way? Let's take a look.

CHAPTER 9

Creating a Culture
of Original Thinkers

W hen it comes to innovation cultures, I see two kinds of companies. The first is the conventional company that works hard to inno- vate. They have a specific group of people tasked with coming up with new ideas. Sometimes they're product managers. It could be a research and development department. They're the PhD engineers. The design thinkers. The subject matter experts of the organization. Or even a team that's specifi- cally been given the "innovation" label. They're quarantined off from the rest of the business so they can focus on coming up with revenue-generating con- cepts. Innovation and the responsibility for it sits squarely on their shoulders.

But if you ask anyone else in a conventional company for new ideas, they say one of two things.

First is "That's not my job."

When there's a group that's specifically tapped for innovation, everyone else believes they're off the hook. They don't have to think about better ways to do their job. There's no reason to look at their work from an outside perspective because that's someone else's responsibility. They show up day after day and do their work in exactly the same way.

The second response people give is "I'm not smart enough" or "I'm not qualified for that."

When you get specific about the qualifications of the team of people responsible for new ideas, you make everyone else think they're dumb. An accountant isn't going to use design thinking to figure out a better job to pay invoices. A human resources rep won't use predictive modeling before trying out a new approach for how he manages meetings. The sophisticated strategies that people use for product and service innovation don't translate into the work that the general employee population does.

It's a tough road when you look at it from the innovation team's perspective as well. I've had heads of innovation tell me they're asked to fix every problem in the company. Those outside of their group—the other 90 percent of the organization—point in their direction when there's a headache to solve because it's not their job or they don't know how to do it. The 10 percent with the official title feel frustrated. While innovation *is* their job, the rest of the employee base expects them to troubleshoot every hurdle along the way. This is because there's not a single, universal definition of what innovation actually *is*. While the innovation team is smart enough to figure things out, they aren't responsible for every problem throughout the entire company. And even if they were, there's no way that they (or even their team) have the bandwidth to solve every dilemma that comes up. They're supposed to work on the products and services the company sells so they can figure out new ways to bring in more revenue. That's where their responsibility stops.

In conventional companies, it's a double-edged sword: Regular employees outside the innovation group don't come to the table with a new idea because they're worried that, somehow, they'll be wrong. They don't want to risk looking stupid. Since it's not part of their job description, they don't want to risk sticking their neck out for fear it will be cut off. That means 90 percent of the employee population is cut out of the innovation process. But the 10 percent who are left get completely overloaded and stretched too thin.

Now, compare this with perpetually innovative companies.

Innovative brands believe that innovation is everyone's business. Each employee has responsibility for big thinking and great ideas. They understand that innovation is more about their company's ability to move quickly than it is about invention, which is why they focus on people. There's a strong belief that everyone is capable of innovation, regardless of their background, experience, or certifications. In perpetually innovative companies, management expects each employee to get creative with how they can solve problems and do their job better in the big picture of the company's business objectives.

> Innovative brands understand that innovation is more about their company's ability to move quickly than it is about invention, which is why they focus on people.

Perpetually innovative companies believe in the democracy of great ideas. They know that you'll never have truly open innovation when you practice closed participation. With a clear message that great ideas are everyone's job, they believe that every person has a responsibility and accountability for coming up with great ideas.

And their expectations pay off handsomely. German construction company Strenger Gruppe invited almost 300 employees to its annual ideas competition. The group was assigned the objective of coming up with ideas to "Be simply the best" to make the company more efficient and customer friendly. The result was more than 150 ideas that will help it maintain its leadership position in its market. UK organic and baby toddler food company Ella's Kitchen launched "Give It a Go." This program gives its employees both time and freedom to broaden the landscape from which they think about their potential within the company. The brand encourages employees to think beyond their roles and look holistically about feeding children. This had employees watching kids' swimming lessons, visiting nurseries, and talking to parents about how they felt about the snacks they fed their kids. It sparked ideas for several innovations, including a snack line called Time Out, which gives parents healthy snack alternatives when they're on the go. It's one of the reasons the company has topped £70 ($90 million) in revenue.

Companies that encourage and support innovation at the individual level generate higher-quality ideas that are faster to implement, and they are better at responding to market and customer demands. That's why they have 5.5 times the revenue growth compared to conventional brands that have an elitist approach to innovation.

Shifting Culture

If leaders want to move people off dead center and create momentum, they need to begin with a powerful, positive force. People believe true innovators are a rare breed. But in reality, people are naturally born original thinkers. But instead of having their instinctive genius conditioned out of them so they conform, they just need the right environment in which to come up with, and raise their hand with, new ideas. And lots of them.

As an innovator in one of the most difficult environments possible—the US Navy—Ben Kohlmann is proof of this.

The military is built around hierarchy, conformity, and following orders. There's a reason for it: People's lives depend on heeding the directives of experienced leaders. Ideas in most businesses don't come with life-or-death consequences, but it can feel that way.

As an instructor and director of flight operations in the Navy, Ben knew that the purpose of a good officer was to win wars. Often, that meant bucking the status quo. In fact, Ben saw that the most successful pilots in combat were the ones who pushed back against authority.

It was something that hit home with him one day as he strolled through San Diego's Balboa Park. Stationed at Miramar, Ben had a new commanding officer in the Marine Air Group, who issued an edict that any of his airmen who stayed out past midnight were required to call and inform him.

"The Navy trusted me to fly a $75 million plane, yet I needed permission to stay out late," Ben lamented. He knew how to think for himself. He just wasn't allowed to.

It sparked an idea for an article he wrote for *Small Wars Journal* titled "The Military Needs More Disruptive Thinkers." In it, Ben laid out his belief for the need to create a military culture in which people with a broad exposure to different areas of expertise come together to solve challenges.

> Our war colleges teach doctrinaire procedures, not critical, creative thinking. They focus primarily on the tactical employment of forces rather than the strategic context those tactics play out in. Where are the courses on trends in physics like chaos theory? Behavioral economics and psychology? Investment strategy? Creating and adapting a dynamic balance sheet? True strategic leaders are generalists who can pull from a variety of interests, not hedgehogs who can only do one thing well.

Ben's article caught the eye of Rear Admiral Terry Kraft, commander of the Navy Warfare Development Command. The NWDC had the task of thinking about the future of warfare, and the members were trying to figure out innovative ways of helping America win new wars. The problem was that the Navy's tactics were stuck in the 1970s. When the rear admiral reached out to Ben, Ben asked the question, what if they took the craziest minds, let them run wild, and came up with ideas? The commander told Ben to put his money where his mouth was.

Ben jump-started the process by becoming one of the founding members of the Chief of Naval Operations' Rapid Innovation Cell. The CRIC depended on senior leaders to support younger recruits. Then, he needed a range of sailors to explore ideas that weren't defined. He took a group of unconventional recruits who had been reprimanded for pushing boundaries and disobeying direct orders. For example, in a *Harvard Business Review* interview, Ben said, "One recruit had been fired from a nuclear submarine for disobeying a commander's order. Another had flat-out refused to go to basic training. Others had yelled at senior flag officers and flouted chains of command by writing public blog posts to express their iconoclastic views." He pointed out that they were all "lone wolves"—until he got hold of them. He wanted these unconventional thinkers to work with each other and senior leadership to challenge deeply rooted assumptions and then generate new ideas.

"People who are passionate about something care about the organization," Ben explained. "We said we'd give them the opportunity to drive change, then gave them the openness and used their energy to build the organization. We didn't have to convince them to care and let them positively express their thoughts. It was about energy management, we redirected it and allowed them to flourish into their natural potential."

He blended these troublemakers with other recruits who had never shown an interest in changing the way things ran. Doing this opened the eyes of the latter group and introduced them to new ways of thinking. Ben had them visit MIT Lincoln Laboratory and other innovation centers. They studied books on innovation.

"The most productive time was the happy hours when we had unconstrained thinking and the group wasn't tied to the traditional Navy," Ben revealed. "There was a collision between tradition and then thinking of things differently that created fireworks."

The Navy didn't have specific objectives for what the CRIC delivered. The commander simply wanted new ideas. He was in a quandary. A state-of-the-art submarine cost upward of $2 billion and 20 years to deliver. Wars in Iran and Afghanistan showed that they were getting beat by $500 techniques.

"Even though we were better funded, the enemy was out-cycling us with new ideas," Ben explained. "The commander wanted new things that were off the shelf."

The commander was the only one who saw he could empower people of a new generation to come to the table with fresh perspectives. If the initiative failed, he didn't see a downside to having experimented. If it succeeded, it gave him a new avenue for disruptive thought. It turned out it was powerfully successful.

For the first time, these original thinkers were encouraged to be provocative and vocal about what they thought. They came up with ways to use 3-D printers on ships and explored using a "robotuna" called the GhostSwimmer, a fish robot, for stealth underwater missions.

Ben pointed out that the culture of the group was everything. "When people discovered their voice, they became unstoppable." As this group found success, they inspired the launch of other rapid-innovation cells in other parts of the military. The success of what Ben's teams accomplished wasn't an isolated incident. Without realizing it, his experiment inspired others to want to become part of the CRIC group and bring their innovative ideas forward.

"This all goes to the people piece," said Ben. "Tech is good, but the people are better. The military and large companies want the application, things they can see. But the more important issue is getting people to think about things differently. When we put the 3D printers on ships, people thought it was great to print things, but the ship's commander was skeptical. A year later he begged us to keep it on board. Not because of what it created, but because of the mindset shifts that happened. They had ideas that they could now print out. Tech is the means to release the potential for humans."

For Ben, the old saying is true: Success begets success. While he was up against an inelastic culture, he found a way to identify and empower the innovators that brought out their greatest strength: Their unconventional thinking. Your efforts may fall short because leaders tap specific people within your company to come up with new ideas, usually a clearly defined innovation or R&D team. Management doesn't let rank-and-file employees take chances with ideas because they assume the best possible innovators are people with rare skills and special gifts. That's a misconception.

> Management doesn't let rank-and-file employees take chances with ideas because they assume the best possible innovators are people with rare skills and special gifts. That's a misconception.

These hotshots can't keep their fire blazing forever. They burn out, and there's no one to step up and fill their spot. It creates a huge stumbling block for the rest of the organization. It's important to realize that underestimating the general population hurts everyone. Most people actually are more than capable of original ideas and successfully rethinking ways to solve problems, but the culture that surrounds them has pounded them into conformity.

Think about the business and financial impact of rethinking how you look at innovation. Getting 10 percent more ideas from a small group can't outpace having a 1 percent increase from the larger employee population. To fight conformity and complacency, you must develop and nurture original thinkers in every corner of the business.

The key to creating a culture of original thinkers—of innovators—starts with champions, the people who are trying to make it happen. At some point there has to be a larger acceptance of the approach by the whole organization. We see that in Ben Kohlmann's experience in the Navy.

The Process in Practice

As we move from people *knowing* how to innovate to them actually *taking action*, you need to realize it doesn't have to come from the top. In fact, this is the biggest stumbling block after people's Brand Detachment Disorder excuses about why innovation can't be done. You've experienced BDD at the corporate level: People say they want innovation and to be a part of it, but they're sitting around waiting for someone higher up to tell them what to do or give them permission to take action. They're afraid they'll get in trouble or that they're not qualified.

Now that you've learned the Perpetual Innovation Process, you no longer have to sit on the sidelines twiddling your thumbs. You don't need an MBA, you don't have to collect a bevy of letters behind your name, and you don't have to earn a fancy certification.

You have a process for coming up with new, great, and reliable ideas on a consistent basis. You can generate and pitch them across any level of your organization. That's exactly why I designed the process the way I did: so anyone at any level can generate and pitch ideas that anyone anywhere in the company can see and appreciate.

Next, let's look at what it takes to spark innovation in your company as an individual.

CHAPTER 10

Innovation at the Individual Level

H ave you ever noticed how creative kids are? Young people see a cardboard box and it becomes a pirate ship. A stump in the woods is now a queen's throne. Tie a swath of cloth around their neck and suddenly they're a superhero.

When's the last time you did that? Have you ever thought about why you stopped doing these things? Does a switch flip for us and we put all the ridiculousness aside? Believe it or not, it turns out that our natural creativity is actually engineered out of us.

In 1968, the deputy director for NASA came to George Land with a problem. George was a general systems scientist who founded a research and consulting institute to study the enhancement of creative performance. The deputy director told George that they had a lot of smart engineers working for them, but they needed a way to root out the most creative ones. NASA wanted to put these creative engineers in groups to tackle its toughest challenges. George and his team came up with such a test, applied it, and the results identified engineers NASA could tap for more creative problem-solving skills.

After thinking about how hard it was for NASA—one of the most innovative organizations in the world—to find creative people, George began to wonder: Where, exactly, does creativity come from? Is it something a person is born with? Do they learn it? He decided to develop a test for creativity that was so simple even children could take it.

With a sample of 1,600 five-year-olds, George dug into the ability of these kids to look at a problem and come up with new, different, and innovative ideas. He retested them when they were 10 and again at age 15. The results were astounding. He found that at age five, 98 percent of children measured at the "genius level" of creativity. By age 10, the number had dropped to 30 percent. Five years later, at age 15, only 12 percent were in the same category. Fast-forward to adulthood, and of the 1 million people George and his team tested over time, only 2 percent of grown-ups ranked as creative savants.

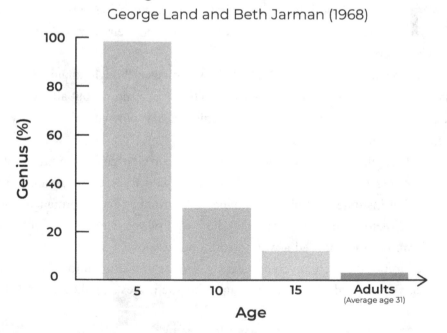

Source: George Land, *The Failure of Success*, TEDx Tucson, YouTube, February 16, 2011.

The challenge that NASA faced in the 1960s is one every business still faces today: How do we solve problems with more innovative thinking? (Remember, creativity and innovation go hand in hand.) If we're born naturally creative, how do we lose that natural genius? It's certainly something that we've learned to forget by the time we climb the corporate ladder.

Take, for example, Michael Brenner. Michael was the vice president of content marketing for SAP—the company's first. In this role, he headed the brand's push into content marketing. With a focus on efficiencies, the marketing structure around him changed nearly every year, and at one point he found himself as the only marketing person surrounded by a team of advertising people.

"I was the bastard child," Michael explained. "I was the only non-advertising person on a team of advertisers."

The group head instituted rigid processes for content approval and publishing. For example, because the culture was KPI-driven, every campaign required a landing page to track user interactions. As brand fell under the same group head, she required everyone to follow the brand guidelines to a T when they created landing pages. She made it clear there was no wiggle room for variance.

However, Michael's job was to cut through the clutter of marketing messages and make his content—and landing pages—stand out so SAP could attract new customers. "I worked with agencies to create innovative landing pages that broke through the clutter and didn't look like everything else. But the brand team's job was to make everything look the same. How can you create something that's innovative that still fits stringent brand guidelines?"

This and other hardline branding processes killed creativity and any chance of fresh, new ideas seeing the light of day. When Michael sat down to meet with his boss about a workaround, the first words out of her mouth were, "We're the place where dreams go to die."

Innovative Companies Start with Innovative People

Innovation in organizations isn't something you write a purchase order for or get through mergers and acquisitions. Businesses need innovators. Michael Brenner was one of those people. At the beginning, however, one individual isn't enough to make an innovative company. You need groups of individuals acting together.

True innovation is something that comes from the employees in your company. If you want an innovative company, then you have to reverse engineer the process down to the one-person-at-a-time level. Innovative companies start with innovative individuals.

If companies expect to create a brighter, customer-centered future, relying on only 2 percent of the workforce to deliver the best ideas isn't feasible—George Land was sure clear about that. Especially if you look at the likelihood that this micro group of people will be able to sustain idea generation and problem solving at scale over the decades of their careers. The road will be cluttered with creative burnouts.

While new, great, and reliable ideas start with people, we're teaching and rewarding the exact skills we need *out* of students and employees. The innovators are the critical thinkers who actively come up with new ideas and solve problems—just like NASA discovered. Businesses need innovators infused throughout the company, because regardless of what size or type of business you're in, nearly every company is looking to improve. The more people you have who can deliver new, great, and reliable ideas consistently, the greater your opportunity for growth.

Think about your own career progression.

You were once fresh out of college, a cheerful 22-year-old excited about what was ahead. Maybe you got a job doing product research for a cement manufacturing company and were full of fabulous ideas. You started pitching stuff, stuff the cement industry had never seen before. Maybe you saw the potential of YouTube and wanted to do a series called "Cement Savants." But your boss said, "Cement buyers don't watch YouTube. But they like bigger bags of our product. Go make bigger bags."

Or maybe your career started out marketing heart catheters. You were excited about changing the medical industry forever. You came up with a sales strategy that was fun and innovative. But your boss said that physicians aren't fun; they're serious. They don't play games; they read research reports and white papers. So, go write a white paper.

Could it be that your first gig was for a forensic accountant? You saw the potential of education as a customer retention technique and were super excited about starting a blog that would knock the socks off prospective customers. And your boss said, "Accountants are left-brained, and they don't like exciting stuff. This will never work and besides, that's not how we do things here. Forensic accountants like free 1-800 numbers to call when they have a question. Make sure the music on hold is perky and that you have a voiceover that mentions our company's name. A lot." So, you looked for perky music.

It felt like every great idea you pitched ended up going back to the same boring things you'd always done.

At 22 you were fresh out of college. Bright-eyed and bushy-tailed. You were excited to change the world with creative ideas. You had a high tolerance for risk and rejection because you didn't have anything to lose. Ideas came to you right and left, and you pitched five great ideas every week. Working the law of averages, you knew that if you swung enough times, you'd get a hit. After a few years, you realized you needed to reign in your creativity a bit. Maybe making the topic of cement a sexy one wasn't something that mattered to anyone else. But you were curious and full of questions, and still excited about pitching ideas.

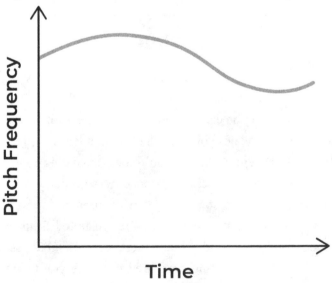

Pitch Frequency as a 22-Year Old

By 32, you've gotten jaded. You know the likelihood of someone saying yes to anything that's massively different is pretty small, but you still hold out hope. You take more time to pitch ideas and send out a lot of feelers. You discreetly mask and then circulate your wacky, yet wildly creative, concept to test the waters. When people say they don't like it, you suck it up and chime in, "Yeah, me neither. I can't believe someone thought that would fly." Pitching new ideas drops to about once every six months, and you are *prrreeeeetty* careful about how "out there" your ideas are.

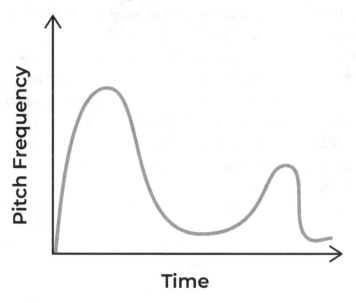

Pitch Frequency as a 32-Year Old

At 42, you have a mortgage. You have kids to put through college. You've built a stable career, and you can see retirement on the horizon. At 42 you only pitch the best ideas—the ones you know have a high likelihood of succeeding, the ones that'll get accepted. At 42, you're only swinging at the slow balls. You're only pitching a new idea about once every other year…and they're really just a continuation of something you've already done and you know people will say yes to. That's because you're frustrated from hearing no to every great idea you pitch. And, to be honest, you're embarrassed about the work that you've ended up doing compared to where you thought you'd be back when you were an idealistic 22-year-old.

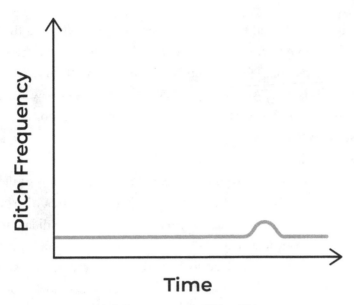

Time

Pitch Frequency as a 42-Year Old

This is what company culture does to people. Over the years, risk-adverse bosses have gotten you to believe that you can't be innovative or do creative work. People love the phrase "In God we trust. Everyone else needs data." Is this really what work has become?

Yes, and we need to "unbecome" it.

But, how do you do that?

Even though you now have a framework for consistently coming up new, great, and reliable ideas with the Perpetual Innovation Process, everyone is different. How you come up with something using the framework has a completely different slant from the person who sits at the desk next to you. You have to understand how you use the process in a way that's unique to you and taps into the natural lens you use to look at the world.

Introducing Citizen Innovators

To bring the level of innovation and creative thought to your work that you yearn for, it's important to understand two distinctions:

1. First is understanding what a role is. This is behavior people assume based on a particular situation. You accept a job for the role of a financial analyst, a CIO, or a vice president of marketing. A role is what you *do*.

2. The second is an archetype. Archetypes are behaviors that're natural for a person. It's why you say, "Let's get Jenny, she's a natural people person." Or, "Where's Christian? He'll know how to map all of this out." An archetype is who you *are* and how you naturally show up in the world. It's your zone of genius, for which people seek you out.

Here's why these distinctions matter.

When you look for a new job, you read through the details of the position description, especially the part that says, "This role requires…" You want to know what behavior the company expects to see in the candidate they eventually hire. However, focusing solely on what people *do* is a big contributor to silos. When everyone is glued to their role and how they're supposed to behave in those situations, that inadvertently creates roadblocks for everyone else. When you're told to "swim in your lane," it means keep your eyes on the role you were hired for and stick to that.

Compare that to archetypes.

Plato once said that your archetype describes "your ideal self." When you embrace who you really are, that's when you're at your best. Archetypes are the secret forces behind all human behavior. They dwell in your unconscious and influence your every move, much of the time without you even knowing it. If you're a natural people person, that's a talent that you take to every role you have throughout your career. If you're a master at weaving stories, you look at the world through that lens.

This gives you an opportunity to rethink how you look at the rigid Kevins, intuitive Yvonnes, and pushy Ernies in your meetings. Can it be that the thing we dread most about them is actually what has the potential to make them an innovation powerhouse?

Yes, it is. And understanding these individual traits is the key to creating highly aligned, collaborative, and innovative teams.

I call these highly original thinkers Citizen Innovators. They're anyone at any level of an organization who plays an active role in the process of consistently coming up with, sharing, and pursuing new, great, and reliable ideas with a specific objective in mind.

> Citizen Innovators are anyone at any level of an organization who plays an active role in the process of consistently coming up with, sharing, and pursuing new, great, and reliable ideas with a specific objective in mind.

As you struggle with the balance of art and science in business today, it's critical to tap into Citizen Innovators. These are the people who will change the way you think of innovation, from product development and business modeling to reinventing healthcare and improving the planet on which we live. They'll be the people knocking on your door with the ideas that can turn into extraordinary outcomes because they understand the power of the Perpetual Innovation Process.

Citizen Innovators represent a shift in the ownership of ideas from the few to the many. These are the people who will tackle problems big and small and repeatedly reinvent their role in business today. When you empower everyone to contribute ideas, you show that not only do they have a necessary role in shaping business; they have an obligation. This is how you democratize innovation and tap into the brilliance of your broader employee base to solve problems you don't realize hold your company back.

Not every Citizen Innovator looks the same, nor should they. Each has their own ideal self or, as Plato calls it, their unique archetype. Understanding your strengths helps bring out your best in your own work and how you use the Perpetual Innovation framework. It affects how you contribute on a team and how you interact with others in your organization. It also affects how well you perform in any role you're in. The most successful Citizen Innovators understand that while they have their own core archetype, it's important to create a balance of perspectives. When they're skilled in the bigger picture of Citizen Innovators, they understand that when they're part of an unbalanced team, they can step into the shoes of other missing archetypes. By doing this, they bring glue to the group, allowing it to shore up a plan so an idea has a greater chance of success. Archetypes aren't tied to job titles or hierarchy, but rather to how people use the framework to bring ideas to the table and contribute to seeing them through to execution.

Following are the six archetypes of Citizen Innovators that make up the most successful teams in the most innovative companies, regardless of size, industry, or location. As you read through them, do you identify with just one of them? Or do you see yourself in several? Some people report that they're a little bit of all of them; does that sound like you? Think about each of the zones of genius and how they may apply to you. This will help you see how the teams you're on might be set up, where and how you naturally contribute or struggle, and why.

1. The Strategist

Zone of Genius: Plan and execute

Strategists love to create a plan and then get things done. They always have an eye for priorities and how to execute things, so they have results to show. Delivering value is at the heart of the Strategist. They readily accept accountability and responsibility for innovation—regardless of their title. Strategists know and understand the bigger business strategy, shepherd work through the process, and out the door. They understand true success requires both a plan and action. They like to teach others to do the same, and people identify Strategists as the go-to people to launch new ideas and bring them to fruition.

When it comes to innovation, the Strategist archetype can see around the corner. They seem to have a sixth sense when it comes to thinking bigger and naturally know the steps to get things done. They like to have concrete plans and to measure and report progress.

However, sometimes they get so caught up in execution that they lose sight of how to bring people along for the ride. Strategists can come across as rigid, egotistical (I know best), aloof, and out of touch. They can be convinced of their own rightness to such a degree that they turn off others and have a hard time convincing them that their ideas have merit.

Examples of successful Strategists include Microsoft founder Bill Gates, Berkshire Hathaway chairman Warren Buffett, and German chancellor Angela Merkel.

2. The Culture Shaper

Zone of Genius: Communicate change

Culture Shapers architect the brand and over-see how it's being expressed. They sculpt the image and perception of innovation and articulate the range of expertise that its people share. With the Culture Shaper comes the rise of the storytellers— the people who create a compelling story arc over a long period of time and then understand how to infuse it into the narrative of the organization. They use it to activate and inspire employee trust, partici-pation, and courage, particularly in times of great transition and change.

When a Culture Shaper connects the dots, they're able to create a compel-ling storyline around change and get people to join forces. They're savvy at helping those around them realize that status quo has become the threat rather than the risk of doing something new. Culture Shapers tap into the storyline of the experience of others to show people the way so that changing habits and deeply engrained behaviors happen with less resistance.

But keep in mind that they can get so caught up in the execution of the story and getting it right that they lose sight of the most important element: people. Their focus on the future leads them to forget that they need to slow down and bring others along for the ride. Culture Shapers can come across as impatient, demanding, and out of touch.

Head of Virgin Group Richard Branson, former Patagonia CEO Rose Mar-cario, and CEO of UK Power Networks Basil Scarsella are all examples of Culture Shapers.

3. The Psychologist

Zone of Genius: Empathy

By smashing the traditional perspective of a highly rational approach to solving problems, the Psychologist understands unstructured innovation. They explore perceptions of an idea from every direction. This is where empathy in business comes into play. What's it like to be the customer of your idea?

What are all the dynamics in how this idea will ultimately play out? What are the emotional ramifica-
tions of this innovation? Psychologists understand
the evolving role of trust not just in innovation but
in business today.

Psychologists are the people who bring the soft
side to innovation. They intuitively see connections
that others miss because they're tuned into how
ideas make people feel and the emotional impact
they have on someone. They may be the most fit of
any of the archetypes because of all the time they've
spent walking in other people's shoes.

But because they can wear their heart on their sleeve, there's days when
they get too hung up on how ideas make others feel. They may struggle with
keeping the bigger picture of innovation front and center because of the people
involved, and they'll get mired down in politics. The phrase they hate to hear
the most? It's not personal, it's business.

Examples of Psychologists include media mogul Oprah Winfrey, research
professor Brené Brown, and Whole Foods CEO John Mackey.

4. The Orchestrator

Zone of Genius: Lead fearlessly

An Orchestrator choreographs the process to
keep things humming. They know how to keep all
the parts and pieces in sync and get things done.
They advocate for the experience of the customer.
They think about how to establish relationships
earlier in the process, with both internal teams and
external customers and partners. Orchestrators
know how to maneuver the political stepping-stones
in every corner of the business. By reaching out to

other functions integrating with them, the Orchestrator also drives relationships and the reputation of innovation within their organization. This is your

linchpin who knows how to build effective consensus.

Orchestrators may seem like the ultimate influencers, but their impact comes from their willingness to push forward with courage. They're a natural at working across departments and levels of people within an organization. Orchestrators are keen on leading without hesitation and decisive when it comes to making decisions. They're willing to have difficult conversations up front so they can avoid hiccups and resistance down the line.

However, their fearless leadership makes them a lone wolf at times, and things can feel piecemeal. Unless they keep their people skills front and center, others may perceive them as being ladder climbers or even manipulative.

Entertainer, businessman, and philanthropist Bono; Pepsi chairman and CEO Indra Nooyi; and Salesforce CEO Marc Benioff are all examples of Orchestrators.

5. The Collaborator

Zone of Genius: Integration

Ideas can never go anywhere by themselves. Innovation relies on collaboration and socialization. Collaborators love to get involved with some or all of the process, help improve ideas, and then champion them. They understand how to capture the attention of people from other groups to excavate blind spots and nurture relationships. This helps them create powerful ideas and increase the chances of success. Collaborators care less about getting personal credit and more about building bonds, so ideas have a greater chance of success.

When a Collaborator's in the groove, they're able to help people see their blind spots. They know how to nurture relationships in ways that make people want to bring their best to the task at hand, which creates cohesion on teams. Collaborators understand that people can create bigger, better things together than when they play the Lone Ranger. They actively look for ways to integrate with others to expand their own abilities and those of the people with whom they work. They are equally good if teams work in person or in remote environments. They prove to be excellent mentors.

But their focus on bringing everyone together can mean they get hung up on the tools they use. Their interest in being open can lead them to over-share, and others to avoid them. As they consistently look to bring people together and integrate ideas, it can mean that their work gets flat over time. They end up going after work that's agreeable by everyone rather than truly innovative.

Examples of powerful Collaborators include Rolling Stones drummer Charlie Watts, director Steven Spielberg, and actor, film producer, and environmentalist Leonardo DiCaprio.

6. The Provocateur

Zone of Genius: Challenge the status quo

These nonconformist thinkers question long-held assumptions and generate highly original ideas. As creative disrupters, they lead the way in coming up with new ideas to create transformation within all areas of the business. Their ability to push past the obvious makes them sustainable and prolific idea generators. Once Provocateurs get in the groove, there's nothing too bizarre to consider.

Provocateurs connect dots quickly and easily and can get impatient with others who don't think on their feet like they do. They can be perceived as difficult to get along with and often rub others the wrong way. They fight organizational inertia with novel thinking and unconventional problem-solving approaches. Provocateurs naturally push against the norm of how people think and consistently ask, "What if?" When they try too hard, their ideas seem over the top and unrealistic. A Provocateur's natural talent in generating ideas can fall short in execution.

Examples of Provocateurs include entertainer Lady Gaga, CEO of SpaceX and Tesla Elon Musk, and the young Swedish climate change activist Greta Thunberg.

If you'd like to find out your archetype, go to www.carlajohnson.co/innova-tionarchetype and take the assessment.

Thousands of people from around the world have taken the archetype assessment. As I look at the results, an interesting story unfolds.

More than half (51 percent) of respondents identify as either Culture Shapers or Psychologists, which makes sense in our more customer-focused world of business. More familiar but near equally populated are the Strategists, Provocateurs, and Collaborators. Strategists are an easily recognized function, and we give credit to the envelope-pushing Provocateurs. Execs have recognized that they need natural Collaborators—the people who know how to reach across silos and integrate work between teams.

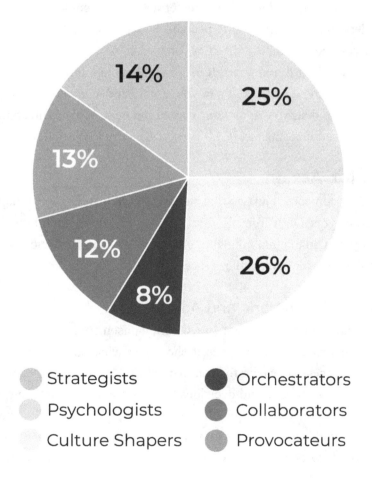

Strategists   Orchestrators

Psychologists   Collaborators

Culture Shapers   Provocateurs

While some innovators say they're ready to lead the charge, drive change, and transform business (even the traditional innovation types), the chart on the previous page shows otherwise. The biggest dearth of natural talent shows up with Orchestrators—the people willing to have the difficult conversations that need to be had in any situation. Avoiding these talks doesn't keep peace; it holds innovation back, hurts people's credibility, fuels passive-aggressive behavior, and keeps people from realizing their highest potential.

Executives at every size company are looking for ways to be more effective with innovation. It's unlikely that any one person will have all the characteristics that original thinking needs. Before you can turn your company into a perpetually innovative organization, you have to understand your own strengths and quirks and how you interact with other people. Once you know and understand yourself, you'll become a dynamic anchor on any team, because your contribution will go beyond your job title and bring out your natural genius. You'll find yourself using the Perpetual Innovation Process as second nature, and the perception of you as a trusted innovator will skyrocket. Once you have that, you're on your way to the next step: architecting highly aligned innovation teams.

Ideas for Action

Maybe your company's just getting started with innovation, or perhaps it has been part of your DNA from the start. Either way, there are things that you, personally, can do to build your chops as a Citizen Innovator and get better at making the Perpetual Innovation Process a habit.

1. Assess, Benchmark, and Adjust

Take the innovation assessment (www.carlajohnson.co/innovationarchetype) to find your archetype. How does it show you what parts of the Perpetual Innovation process are easier for you than others? How do you see it play out in your everyday actions and decisions? Are you in a role that weighs down on how you naturally show up in the world? Now, guess the archetypes of the people you work with most. Once you know your archetype and the people around you, how does it change the dynamics of your relationship? Does it make you more willing to share ideas or champion change? How can you shore up their weak spots with what comes natural to you and vice versa? Take note of this: Which archetype compliments your style will change based on the situation in which you find yourself.

2. Think Big. Start Small.

You might not realize it, but you're in a serious rut. You're used to your daily routine and focusing on efficiency. That means plenty of things have gone on autopilot.

It feels overwhelming to think about trying to change the direction of your organization all at once or all by yourself. I had a boss caution me against this early in my career: "You'll get your arms ripped off if you try to redirect the ship too fast," he warned.

Start first with the smallest of things you regularly do: observing the world around you. For example, do you have a weekly meeting with your team or sit in on another department? Change the chair that you usually sit in. This does two things. First is that it changes your own frame of reference—the lighting is different, your view is different, the chair you're sitting on or the wall you lean against is different. That puts your nervous system on alert and says you need to pay attention. You'll heighten your senses and all of a sudden start noticing things that you didn't before.

The second thing is that it creates a ripple effect. Others have to take a different seat, and that makes them perk up. What happened? Why did Judy sit someplace else? Their whole energy changes, and one by one, everyone becomes more present and aware. They no longer move mechanically through the meetings.

Or slow down and take a fresh look at the little details of your job. My husband used to work at Omaha Steaks. One of the meat cutters on the production floor started to pay attention to how much tape he used to seal boxes of steaks. One day he decided to see if, instead of closing a box shut by running tape all the way around it, would it work to stop the tape halfway down the sides? Turns out, he could. Just by him asking, "I wonder if I can do something different? I wonder if I can change that?" he ended up saving the company thousands of dollars a year just in tape. It started by taking the smallest step of observing the world around him.

3. Dedicate Time

People say you have to make time for innovation. I disagree. If you're going to become a Perpetual Innovator, you make it a priority. "Making" time implies that we can create more of something. We only have so many hours in the day and the successful innovators commit to the practice.

The only thing that stands between a good idea and a great idea is time. When you're under a deadline, your focus is so narrow that you can't draw from a diverse pool of stimuli to help you solve problems. It's like kinking a hose and expecting more water to come out when you have to fight a fire. That's why ideas pop into your head in the shower, when you're taking a run, in the middle of the night, or when you're doing something utterly mundane. Your brain has room to travel on its nonlinear problem-solving path.

What gets scheduled gets done. Set aside an hour a week to review some of the observations you took or dots you've connected. What ideas come to mind? How do they coincide with other ideas you're working on? Do they inspire you to reach out to a particular person and get their input? Giving your brain dedicated time to look for ways to make ideas better trains it how to perform. Just like learning any new skill, when you slow the process down from the get-go, you're able to detect the nuances. Then, as you become more proficient, you'll preform faster and more efficiently when you're under the pressure of a deadline.

4. Embrace Monotasking

People brag about their ability to multitask. But the more balls you try to keep in the air at once, the harder it is to bring out your best ideas. In fact, multitasking can decrease your productivity by a whopping 40 percent!

How many times have you gone through a meeting and then needed to have someone fill you in on the details later? That's because you were physically there but mentally someplace else. You weren't productive in either situation. If you're in a meeting that needs original thinking, you have to be fully present.

If you're constantly preoccupied, you won't be able to follow through with the Perpetual Innovation Process. Trying to apply it to get better results for your client project or your boss's assignment will fail miserably. Multitasking kills the practice. Your mind needs time to settle and relax before it can take in details during the observation step. Remember, the more dots you collect during that step, the more rich and varied constellations you'll have later.

Instead of trying to do too much at once, practice monotasking—doing only one thing at a time and with deep focus. It lets your brain fully focus on one thing and gives it breadth and depth to expand. That's when ideas pop into your head, and you come up with your brilliant ideas. Believe me, in the tech-focused, overcommitted world in which we live, this isn't as easy as it sounds. Practicing this will help you slow down your mind, become more aware of the world around you, and be present in the moment. This is big stuff when it comes to building your innovation chops. You brain needs training so it can perform just like your body does.

5. Reframe Failure

We have a serious hang-up with failure, but it makes sense. From the time we're wee ones, adults hover about, shielding us from mistakes. Don't step in the puddle, you'll get wet. Color inside the lines, it looks better. The sky's blue, not orange. Parents and teachers shroud us with messages of be careful, be careful, be careful.

In her Harvard commencement speech, *Harry Potter* author J. K. Rowling said, "It is impossible to live without failing at something, unless you live so cautiously that you might as well not have lived at all—in which case, you fail by default." If you want to become a successful innovator, you have to accept that not everything will work out like you planned. Think back to the Generate step. Your purpose was to come up with as many ideas as you could, because not all of them will fly. More than you want to admit will die in committee. Some won't have the right timing. Still others just won't make the cut because they simply won't turn out to be reliable ideas. You're guaranteed to have some level of failure. How do you deal with that?

The first is change your lingo. The word *failure* makes people shudder. Instead of saying you failed, repackage it and explain that you tested a couple of ideas, and here's what you learned. That not only eases your fears of delivering a not-so-successful message; it perks up your listeners' ears. People like to know what you learned because it may help them get better at something they do. Lessons have a broad appeal.

Testing helps you build momentum for change by lowering the level of perceived risk people have. Talking about a test opens up room for something to happen, for change. It lets people know that you can always go back to how things were if things don't work out. That makes trying something new less permanent. Try a small test for two weeks, and then get back together and talk about what happened. Did it work? Can you massage what you're testing to get better results? Or do you really need to go back to how things were?

Whatever you try may not be the change you needed. But the mere process of trying shakes the system enough to create momentum for something new to happen.

CHAPTER 11

Innovation at the Team Level

I n one of the episodes of the US version of the comedy series *The Office,* Michael Scott rushes into the scene, demanding everyone give him ideas. As the regional manager of the Scranton branch of Dunder Mifflin Paper Company, he has a reputation for his narcissistic behavior as a supervisor.

On his way into the building that day, Michael saw wet cement in front of the building. He magnifies the situation, telling his employees that one of his lifelong dreams is to leave a legacy in cement. Time is of the essence, he insists, the cement's drying. He needs ideas, lots of them—and good ones— about what imprint to leave that uniquely and memorably represents him.

Kevin, the slow, dim-witted accountant, surprisingly comes up with the first suggestion. "Write your initials," he says with a smug smile to the rest of the staff before Michael shoots down his idea. "No, some idiot named Mark Greg Sputnik will claim credit for it."

Next up is Phyllis from sales. She remembers something from her child-hood and tries to connect the dots. She thinks out loud but takes too much time and Michael loses patience. His annoyance makes her forget what she was thinking about, and she emotionally withdraws.

Then, eager-to-please Andy comes up with a twist by suggesting Michael draw something. "It says more than words," before Michael cuts him off with "Nooooo…NNNNNOOOOO! Give me something *good*."

Flighty Kelly goes off on a tangent trying to tell her idea. Pam the receptionist has to translate it into something relevant for the challenge at hand—leave his handprints in the cement like celebrities do outside the Chinese Theater in Los Angeles.

That peaks Michael's interest. "I love it!"

Then Jim, the office prankster, throws out the most radical idea—a *real* celebrity would leave an imprint of his face in the cement. This works beautifully because not only is it a unique idea, Jim knows he can get Michael to do something outrageous by stroking his ego.

At this point, Oscar—the only rational one in the group—tries to point out that submerging one's face in wet cement isn't safe. But Michael will hear none of it because he's already sold on the idea. The more dangerous it sounds, the more he loves it.

In the midst of all of this is Michael's toady, Dwight. He doesn't offer up any ideas, but he's engaged with excitement, a smile spread across his face. He's the first one to run after his idol when they go downstairs. In the next scene, Michael has a straw taped to his face, presumably to allow him to breathe, and plastic wrap covers his hair. Dwight applies Vaseline to Michael's face, so the cement doesn't stick to it.

Michael leans forward as Dwight applies pressure to the back of his head to make a good imprint into the wet cement. After a few seconds, Dwight needs help to get Michael's face out, and the group lends a hand.

At the end of the scene we see Michael's faceprint in the cement—an unrecognizable pit at the intersection of four squares in the sidewalk. Yet another failed attempt for Michael to leave a brilliant legacy.

What Michael put his employees through is the same experience that you've been put through a thousand times—a boss or a client has a deadline and demands brilliant ideas on a moment's notice. As idea after idea is thrown out, they're rejected. Deep down, people decide to keep their mouth shut next time, they resent the person in charge, trust tanks, and egos drive decision making. A voice of reason gets dismissed as too conservative, and the end result is ridiculous.

The Battle for Brilliance

Companies need ideas. A lot of ideas. You need them for strategic plans. For campaigns. For products. Services. Meeting themes. Growth strategies. Customer retention. The list is endless.

Team innovation is the backbone of every successful company. It's what sets a business apart from the competition and helps it grow and prosper. Getting your staff to think creatively isn't always easy, though. In a survey by Robert Half, 35 percent of chief financial officers said the greatest roadblock to organizational breakthroughs is a lack of innovative ideas. Executives polled also cited excessive bureaucracy (24 percent) and being bogged down with daily tasks or putting out fires (20 percent) as other major barriers.

When we need an idea, the situation isn't much different from that of Michael Scott in *The Office*. Someone in a leadership position circles the wagons, and there's a mass gathering in which coming up with something "fresh, new, and different" is the point of it all. People at every level have experienced the pain of pursuing new ideas through brainstorming sessions. One of the most soul-crushing things a person can get in their inbox is a meeting invitation for a brainstorming session. People know they're cesspools of inefficiency filled with egocentric ladder climbers delighted to have a captive audience.

The result? Some attendees remain stone-faced throughout the entire session. Others contribute sporadically. And there are those few but mighty who loudly dominate with their pet ideas and not-so-hidden agendas. Ideas pop up randomly—some are intriguing, but most are ridiculous—but because the session doesn't have any process or rules, little momentum builds around any of them.

At the end of the day, instead of leaving with an experience that feels fulfilling and productive, people lament how much further behind they are in work. And besides, even if a good idea did come out of a brainstorm, it's not like it will go anywhere anyway.

Alex Osborn's Rules for Brainstorming

Ironically, brainstorming was created to solve the problems we still face today with fresh thinking. In 1941, Madison Avenue advertising executive Alex Osborn found that his employees were having a hard time coming up with new ideas for ad campaigns. He saw that conventional business meetings inhibited the creation of new ideas. Rather than having his people work as solo thinkers, he put them in groups and proposed some rules designed to help stimulate them. These rules gave people the freedom of mind and action to spark off and reveal new ideas.

Alex described brainstorming as a technique that a group uses to find a solution for a specific problem by coming up with as many spontaneous ideas as people can come up with. He had four general rules, and he found that when people followed them, teams created a lot more ideas. They reduced people's natural inhibitions—inhibitions that kept them from volunteering ideas they felt others would consider "wrong" or "stupid." Alex also found that generating "silly" ideas could spark off very useful ones because they changed the way people thought—all with these simple rules:

1. Go for Quantity

When you go for the numbers, it forces you to think about possibilities from many different directions. When you use divergent thinking, you see connections that aren't obvious, and random ideas begin popping into your head. This is exactly what you want. The more ideas you have, the better chances that one of them will eventually lead to a great idea—quantity equals quality. This is critical, and Osborne knew from his advertising work that people tend to settle and stop creating ideas when the first good option pops up.

For teams, it's important to never feel like you're settling for a concept simply because you can't think of a better one. And, let's be honest. When there's the pressure of a deadline, or you just want to move on to the next step, you get lazy. You don't push through the couple of good ideas to get to the truly great ones. It's a numbers game—the more ideas a team generates, the bigger the chance of producing a radical and effective idea.

In the bigger picture, the time that teams spend up front generating as many ideas as possible is minor compared to the time you need to take to move the idea into development and execution.

Here's an example of why it's so important to come up with as many ideas as possible.

A pottery teacher split her class into two halves.

To the first half she said, "You will spend the semester studying pottery, planning, designing, and creating your perfect pot. At the end of the semester, we'll have a competition to see whose pot is the best."

To the other half she said, "You will spend your semester making lots of pots. Your grade will be based on the number of completed pots you finish. At the end of the semester, you'll also have the opportunity to enter your best pot into a competition."

The first half of the class threw themselves into researching, planning, and design. Then they set about creating their one perfect pot for the competition.

The second half of the class immediately grabbed fistfuls of clay and started churning out pots. They made big ones, small ones, simple ones, and intricately detailed ones. Their muscles ached for weeks because of the strength they built by having to throw so many pots.

At the end of class, both groups entered their best work into the competition. Once the votes were tallied, all of the best pots came from the team that was tasked with producing as many pots as they could. What they learned from making so many different samples helped them become significantly better potters than the other students who set out to make the single most perfect pot.

2. Withhold Criticism

This might be the hardest one. We all have that inner critic in our heads that tells us whatever we're doing is wrong. In brainstorming sessions, it's easy to project that. Instead of the idea, these comments are seen (whether true or not) as judgment about the person, not the idea. That activates the inner critic in other people. In a short amount of time, people's body language changes and they become defensive, skeptical, or pessimistic. The energy of the group tanks, and new suggestions are met with a death sentence. This is why anything that whiffs of judgment or criticism of the ideas people generate should be put on hold. There's a time for that later in the vetting process. Instead, people should focus on extending or adding to ideas. By suspending judgment, participants will feel free to talk about the really wacky concepts.

3. Welcome Wild Ideas

To get a good, long list of suggestions, encourage wild ideas. Interestingly, what can seem like the norm in your day-to-day life can sound kooky to someone else and spark a new thought. Do you play the jug in a backyard band? Maybe that's just the spark of genius for your next employee recruitment campaign. I worked with a client who started with a wacky observation about men's facial haircare that turned into a highly successful customer portal. A lot of great ideas can be generated by looking at anything from new perspectives and holding back all your judgy thoughts. Sometimes it takes the crazy to pave the path to the enlightened.

4. Combine and Improve Ideas

In the Perpetual Innovation Process, you learned how to look for dots and then connect them in different ways to create constellations. Alex believed that instead of criticizing ideas, people need to look for ways to improve and evolve them—the $1 + 1 = 3$ philosophy. This stimulates building ideas through association. For example, the Scottish organization Dementia Dog was the result of a group of design students from the Glasgow School of Art. They came up with the idea of using trained assistance dogs to help care for people with dementia by combining the services of Alzheimer Scotland, Dogs for the Disabled, and Guide Dogs UK. English inventor Edwin Budding got the idea for the lawnmower after seeing a machine in a cloth mill that used a cutting cylinder. He combined that with how people used a scythe to cut grass and voilà! We now have a machine to make Saturday-morning lawncare that much easier.

Since Alex introduced brainstorming in 1941, it's spread throughout the world. Most educated managers know it but, sadly, apply it poorly. And that's why it doesn't work. While we have the idealized outcomes that will make us look like creative geniuses, we all know it doesn't actually work like that.

In fact, bad brainstorming is worse than no brainstorming. The whole idea of bringing new ideas to the table in this way is to spark inspiration. But that's not how things work out. They're rife with politics, hidden agendas, and favoritism. If you don't have to subject your team to all of this, why would you?

Bad brainstorming destroys the morale and creative confidence of the people involved. Poor sessions lead to things such as:

- Making teams believe they aren't creative because they didn't come up with any radical ideas.
- Destroying people's faith in the idea-generating process. This could ruin any future chances of making the organization innovative.
- Making staff scared to voice their ideas because they were criticized in a session.
- Alienating staff if their managers pressure them into participating in a poorly supervised session without a friendly, critical-free environment.
- Making brainstorming sessions a time to be dreaded if they focus on the individual performance of people.

Power in the People

The biggest barrier to people's great ideas is people themselves. When push comes to shove and budgets get cut, what does your boss tell you? You need to do more with less.

This is when building a culture of Citizen Innovators comes into play. As you'll remember from the last chapter, each of the archetypes—Strategist, Culture Shaper, Psychologist, Orchestrator, Collaborator, and Provocateur—has their zone of genius, a way of looking at the world as well as the Perpetual Innovation Process, that's different from the others. When you're confident in yourself and what you bring to the table, you not only deliver your best work; you'll help others on your team do the same. Confidence in your own archetype affects how you look at and interact with the other five. Understanding this is the backbone to building highly aligned teams and consistently coming up with new, great, and reliable ideas, because when you understand this dynamic, you'll never be forced to do more with less, but you'll be able to deliver extraordinary things with the people you already have.

You and I probably don't know each other, and we may never meet. But I do know this about you: You don't create your best work by yourself. It's always been when you were part of a highly aligned team. When you were part of this kind of group, you couldn't wait to get out of bed and get to work. This is because you knew you were going to accomplish great things—together. You were proud of the innovative, high-quality work you did. And you compare every other team you've ever been a part of to that one. It takes a great team to deliver extraordinary results.

It's been true throughout history. It took 39 people to write the United States Declaration of Independence. Walt Disney relied on a team of nine animators to make his visions come true. Three astronauts landed on the moon. There were four Beatles. It took 25 Chicago Cubs to win the World Series after a 108-year dry spell. Heck, even Jesus had 12 disciples.

The strength of bringing people together to innovate as a team is that each person brings their own experiences. They make different observations based on how they see the world and what they notice. You may want more creativity, but your ideas will only stretch as far as your team's experience.

Teams are more innovative when managers expect people to innovate, support them when their attempts don't work out the way they planned, and recognize and reward new ideas and the people who implement them. This means encouraging risk and expecting failures. Keep in mind that support for innovation is crucial even if you don't see results right away. It can't always be directly tied to revenue. Sometimes its six degrees of separation from the money, but it takes stick-to-itiveness for innovation to take hold and have an impact on teams and how they perform.

No one person has all the capabilities needed to make innovation a success—it's a team sport. For projects to succeed, they have to be well-constructed with the right combination of talent, not just technical skills but a balance of the six archetypes of the Citizen Innovators.

Ideas for Action

New teams struggle to gel because they've been asked to perform in ways they aren't conditioned to do. In a band, every person has their own expertise, and they practice on their own. As I talked about in the previous chapter, there are a lot of exercises that you can—and should—do as individual Citizen Innovators. That's the backbone for coming together and becoming a high-contributing, innovative team member.

Now that you understand the balance of archetypes on your team, there's plenty you need to think about with team culture. One reason people don't like team brainstorming sessions is because they spend hours upon hours together, but nothing comes out of them. You now have the power to change all of that. And here's some things you can use to change how teams, and the people on them, look at innovation.

1. Go for the Worst, First

Let's face it, no one wants to deal with the awkward silence that comes from shouting out a horrible idea. Some people worry about sounding stupid if they pitch ideas that aren't well thought-out. Others are especially apprehensive when people in power positions join in the exercise. This stunts confidence, creativity, and productivity in teams.

Start your together time by countering that fear and going for the low—challenge the team to come up with the worst ideas they can think of first. Doing this creates two important dynamics.

First, it gets people to warm up and laugh. And laughter is the best inspiration for great ideas. Research from MIT showed that group participants who took a cartoon caption humor test and a product brainstorming test produced 20 percent more ideas and 25 percent more *creative* product ideas than professional product designers.

Second, it gets ideas going. Many great ideas started out as bad ones. Laughter can help people solve problems that need innovative answers by making it easier to think more broadly and associate ideas and relationships more freely. People in a lighter mood experience more eureka moments and greater inspiration.

The best idea times for teams come when everyone feels comfortable throwing out *all* of their thoughts, regardless of whether or not they're gold. Starting with the worst means things can only get better from there.

2. Start with Singles. Work Toward Doubles.

Many people assume that the dynamics of group idea generation is always the way to go. Numerous studies support the exact opposite. An article in the *Journal of Creative Behavior* says that "Groups of individuals generating ideas in isolation (nominal groups) generated more ideas and more original ideas and were more likely to select original ideas during the group decision phase than interactive group brainstormers." One way to support this is to have team members come up with ideas on their own before the group session. It can be as simple as sending out the challenge before the meeting and letting everyone write down ideas, without input from others, before everyone comes together to talk them through. Or you can do something like hang a big sheet of paper in a central area like a break room, office lobby, or high-traffic hallway and let people write or draw things before the meeting.

Giving people the chance to passively brainstorm before your meeting begins helps balance the tension between introverts and extroverts. To introverts, an idea session can make them feel like they can't get a word in edgewise as extroverts feed off each other's energy. On the flip side, extroverts can feel they're doing all the work and can't squeeze a peep out of the introverts. Giving people a chance to work both individually and in groups helps bring out the creative strengths of both personalities.

3. Get Out of the Office

You can't be creative in the same conference room where you have your performance review or listen to a town hall on the company's financial performance. In fact, switching up your physical environment isn't just a fun change of pace; it can actually affect the way your brain works. Neurobiologists believe rich, stimulating environments could speed up the rate at which the human brain creates new neurons and neural connections. That means *where* you host your team meetings and pitch sessions can have an effect on the ideas your team comes up with.

Try holding get-togethers in rooms that aren't associated with regular group get togethers. If you can't change the room itself, try changing something *about* the environment to stimulate the brain, such as rearranging the chairs or putting bright, vibrant pictures on the walls. Another idea is to have your team stand up and walk around while meeting to encourage fluid creativity.

Get a change of scene. When you were a kid in school, did you ever have class outside? If you have a rooftop deck, think about having meetings there. Or look for a park that's within walking distance. What if you broke up the afternoon by going to a trendy coffeeshop and got away from the cube farms and buzzing fluorescent lights of the office? If you're bringing people together from several office locations, switch up the location where you meet so things feel fresh. If you really have money in the budget, skip the country. Columbia Business School professor Adam Galinsky found that international travel does a lot for your ability to jump between different ideas and connect the dots between them, both of which are fundamental to innovative thinking. A big part of this is to immerse yourself in the local culture. Adam found that there's a clear correlation at 270 high-end fashion houses between the experiences designers had in other countries and their creative output.

4. Kill a Stupid Rule

There's always some ridiculous rule that holds you back. Here's your chance to take it off your excuses list and simplify your innovative process.

Ideally, get together with people from different departments, and divide them into groups of two or three people each. Then, give each group 10 minutes to answer this question: If you could kill or change all the stupid rules that get in the way of being more creative or innovative, what would they be and how would you do it?

Now, sit back and watch the sparks fly!

Once the teams are done coming up with solutions to "stupid rules," have each team pick out a single favorite to write down on a sticky note. Then, have each team put that sticky note on a grid that uses two axes:

1. Ease of implementation
2. Expected degree of impact

After the sticky notes are all up, talk this through with everyone. If there are things that legitimately are rules for the sake of rules, be prepared to kill some of them on the spot. Showing a willingness to change does a lot to put credibility behind the ideas people come up with and your willingness to change. Remember, a huge part of innovation is consistently looking at how you can keep things simple.

5. Use the One-Question Survey

Empathy expert and marketing executive Michael Brenner uses one question that clears the decks and paves the way for teams to have a powerful impact through innovation: Does my manager support the ideas of my team?"

By using it, Michael has seen an overnight culture change in organizations, because it told managers that ideas and innovation are important to teams. It also let leaders know that their job wasn't to tell people what to do but rather to get feedback from front-line employees who really know what customers want.

The second aspect is that it told team members that their ideas were valuable. With that, employee engagement can jump significantly. In fact, one company Michael worked with experienced a 20 percent jump in just one quarter.

CHAPTER 12

Innovation at the Corporate Level

I t's happened to all of us. We've missed the window to feed the meter and ended up with an annoying parking ticket. A sudden storm hit, and we got drenched in the rain between the garage and the concert venue. Or we've been late to an important interview because we couldn't find a %$*&#! parking spot!

When it comes to parking, "innovation" isn't an image that readily pops into our heads. Instead, it's visions of asphalt slabs and concrete boxes. It's cars circling the block…again…fingers crossed for that elusive open slot.

That's where ParkMobile comes in.

ParkMobile was founded in 2008 to give people an option to find and pay for parking right from their phone using an app. Today, the company serves 400 cities, including eight of the top 10 US urban areas. The growth of the company has come from its ability to build a product that's right for the market, which is how they've grown to more than 18 million users.

Innovation has been at the heart of the company from the very beginning. It took a big jump, though, when chief technology officer Matt Ball came on board in July 2018 and launched the first Innovation Week at the end of that year.

"Our approach has been broad-based across the company," said chief marketing officer Jeff Perkins. "We invited every team in the business to be a part of one week that just focused on innovation. Whether they were in finance, engineering, customer service, we said you can be a part of innovative ideas."

ParkMobile's support of Citizen Innovators flies in the face of many brands' approaches. Jeff explained the backstory: "I've seen companies create innovation labs or buy a place in a tech center. Or there's an innovation lab that sits within the corporate headquarters. Both always end badly. If there's only a few people focusing on innovation, what's everyone else doing? It doesn't bring the rest of the company along with them, and it creates resentment. The goal isn't to create an innovation island, but to get great ideas to come out of all parts of the business."

Matt knew he needed to draw out new ideas in the IT and engineering department and wanted to set the tone right off the bat. His intent was to give his team a week in which they worked on nothing to do with the core business and everything that led to the future of the company and the parking industry.

In planning the week, Matt and Jeff asked people on the IT and engineering team to create a list of projects to work on. These teams then recruited others outside their department to join them. This worked because some employees were more comfortable contributing than leading. It created a way for everyone to be a part of innovation, because they drew from their background and their on-the-job know-how.

By tapping into the entire base of Citizen Innovators, ParkMobile harnessed the collective genius of the organization. While the myth of innovation is that it has to be on the scale of a Tesla, a drone, or a flying car, Jeff and Matt knew it could be the smallest of things—it simply needed to make an impact.

When it came time to present ideas, employees showcased their projects, which built excitement about their potential and the impact they could have. Teams went in front of a group of judges, which included the ParkMobile leadership team, internal employees, and surprise guests, and pitched their ideas.

During their pitch, each team had to explain how they set up the problem they solved, show how the solution solved that problem, and how it impacted ParkMobile. Then they had to sell the judges on why their solution was innovative based on predetermined criteria such as:

- Is it big and transformational? Or is it smaller and has a significant impact?
- Is it realistic? Can we execute and market it?
- How big of an opportunity is this for our company? Will we have a significant upside?
- What's the coolness factor? Would employees and customers get excited about it?

The pitches were all over the board, from building an app for the Apple Watch to voice recognition for Alexa. One woman in the finance department pitched an idea for how her team collected and reconciled data. She had seen that at month end, she had to pull data from different financial sources, dedupe and clean it, then send it to someone else on her team to reconcile. During innovation week she taught herself how to program in the R language and automate it. The woman took a two-week process that required 40 human hours and turned it into a 10-minute automated tool. Her idea relieved her and her team of miserable, repetitive work and freed them up for things that were more interesting to them and valuable to the company.

"We often think of innovation as something that changes the world," pointed out Jeff, "but she changed the world of finance by dealing with the slog. The fact that someone from finance received recognition set the tone that innovation comes from anywhere. It isn't just what and how you bring something to market. It's also about the operational efficiencies that make you better as a company, so you can move faster and get more done."

> "Innovation comes from anywhere. It isn't just what and how you bring something to market. It's also about the operational efficiencies that make you better as a company, so you can move faster and get more done."
>
> —Jeff Perkins, chief marketing officer, ParkMobile

In looking at the overall culture of ParkMobile and their approach to Innovation Week, there are several reasons why it's so successful. Whether you're a large, legacy corporation, a freshly minted start-up, or somewhere in between, these lessons are universally applicable.

First is that the focus on innovation comes from the top. Jeff explained, "We're fortunate to have a CEO who's highly innovative, has a well-defined vision for the company, and where he wants it to go. That's why he pushes hard on every team to be as innovative as possible and made it a core competency of the entire company."

Second, leadership has infused innovation throughout every level of the company as a way to serve customers. ParkMobile knows its place in the life of its customers—they're a parking app, not a lifestyle app. But by constantly putting their customers first, they've been able to remove friction for people using it to park, help their city administrator customers make parking easy for residents, and help government organizations manage the process of payment and future planning.

Third is dedicated time for innovation. "In many businesses, management wouldn't have allowed everyone to take a week off," Jeff said. "Or they'd say do your day job on top of it. But we've seen big returns from this. People appreciate it and it was the highlight of the year. It gave people a chance to show what they can really do when they're not encumbered with the fire drills of the day." It shows in the feedback from everyone, starting with the top of the company. CEO Jon Ziglar explains,

> Innovation Week is really important for ParkMobile. It's a chance for all of our folks to get together and spend time thinking about what they would do for the business. We've got incredibly dynamic and interesting people with great ideas. Giving them the free rein to create without restrictions is a great thing for us, and ultimately, it's a great thing for our clients.

Product manager Joy Guerin says,

> Innovation Week is a great opportunity for the engineers, the product managers, and really anyone at ParkMobile to get involved with

new ideas…the ideas that are just floating around in our minds, the what-if.

Jamaal Hutchinson, a software development engineer, adds,
> Innovation Week gives us the opportunity to create something that is important to us and really makes an impact.

Innovation Week is a reprieve from the grind of day-to-day work. Granted, it's the nature of the beast to have to do repetitive work and fix bugs. But by giving people an opportunity to unplug from the drudgery, you give them space to take on the things they're most excited about, like trying out a new technology they saw at a conference or an approach for how to build a relationship with a customer. It's made Innovation Week an event that people now look forward to and get excited to be a part of, turning it into a real morale booster.

Fourth comes an awareness of highly aligned teams built on Citizen Innovators. People are welcome to join a group where they see they have a unique perspective or talent to add. It adds richness to the process as well as the ideas the team comes up with because people work with others they don't normally.

There's a lot of cross-pollination happening. For example, someone from human resources joined the tech team and created a PowerPoint for their pitch because none of the developers knew how. It helps break down silos and creates more connections. It also helps that the executive team shows its commitment by being active participants. For some employees, this is the only chance they get to work shoulder-to-shoulder with someone from the C-suite.

Last is setting high-quality objectives so the problem is crystal clear to everyone. Jeff pointed out that this came to light during the pitch stage. The teams that won were the best at defining the problem and then bringing it back to the experience of the users, whether that was a customer or something that internal people face.

"With innovation, having strong storytelling skills about the why, not just what your product does, is critical. You have to build the drama around the problem and then put it into the context of your customer. That's crucial to getting people on board with the idea you're trying to sell. At the end of the day, innovation is a sales job of your idea," said Jeff.

Navigating Hurdles

While Jeff, Matt, and the rest of the ParkMobile executive team may not realize it, one of the dependencies of their level of innovation is their ability to balance Citizen Innovators across departments and teams. You've seen why it matters to bring out the full potential of these archetypes in their individual work, and how, together, they create robust, high-performing teams. Park-Mobile shows what can happen when you have a culture that appreciates the natural genius of everyone and then lets them loose to root out, clarify, and solve problems.

Crowdsourcing new ideas in this way has measurable outcomes. In Planview Spigit's *The 2019 State of Crowdsourced Innovation* report, the authors point out specific benefits that came from innovation programs that crowdsourced ideas:

- Cost savings of $300,000 in the first year.
- Launched an entirely new line of business.
- Improved cash flow.
- Increased employee Net Promoter Scores, which gauges employee satisfaction.
- Improved diversity, equity, and inclusion in idea development.

However, when a company gets to a certain size, it starts to lose its appetite for risk across all areas of the business. And the bigger the company gets, the more risk-averse it gets, even if it had innovation wired into its original DNA.

Big companies are all about consensus building. And, as in life, when do big groups of people agree on most anything? They don't. So, what things tend to get the most agreement? The things that nearly everybody can agree on—the stuff in the middle, which isn't too extreme in thinking, one way or the other. That's why big ideas get passed over for simple iterations of things already proven to work. It's simply easier and less frustrating to build consensus.

One thing that holds innovation back in a world of approvals, governance, and corporate compliance is the fear of failure. That's why bosses insist you bring proof that your ideas will work before you're ever allowed to take your first teetering steps. This line of thinking creates an illusion of rationale: *If I can put enough numbers behind it, of course it's going to work.* (Or at least you can convince someone it will.) By its very nature, innovation involves risk because it's about doing something that's never been done before. Whether it's arrogance or ignorance, this approach is a complete waste of time and resources, yet it's one that people give lots of fist pumps to.

The fear of failing at something—of doing it wrong, looking foolish, or not meeting expectations—paralyzes you. You've been conditioned to think that introducing a new idea is a career-limiting move unless you can prove ahead of time that it will succeed. This is a reaction to how tolerant a corporate culture is to change. But the fear of failure hurts innovation because it buries mistakes you can learn from, smothers new ideas, and avoids risky concepts.

If you're an MBA-trained manager or executive, odds are you were never, at any point in your educational or professional career, given permission to fail, even on a "little bet." Your parents wanted you to achieve, achieve, achieve—in sports, the classroom, scouting, or work. Your teachers penalized you for having the "wrong" answers and knocked your grades down if you were imperfect, according to however your adult figures defined perfection. In university, you took electives that helped boost your GPA. Class projects went right down the middle because there was less risk of fallout from your professor that could affect your class rank. In the same way, modern management is still based on its ability to mitigate risks and prevent mistakes, not innovate.

We see this play out even so far as how companies hire. Start-ups aim for a specific type of Citizen Innovator, particularly the idea-generating Provocateurs and the Orchestrators as fearless leaders. Human resources, on the other hand, looks for different kinds of Citizen Innovators, the Collaborators and Psychologists. But as companies grow, they build a formal HR department. And HR directors are all about avoiding risk when it comes to hiring. They shift toward the middle and bring people on board who won't ruffle feathers. That leads to a culture that's very different from the one that the original Provocateurs and Orchestrators signed up for. And it creates two problems. First is that you lose a lot of the top-tier innovators. Second, you hire a bunch of people who all think and act the same. People aren't encouraged, much less rewarded, for thinking outside the box.

Nine times out of ten, a big company prefers to hire internally, with junior-level people rising up through the ranks into more senior positions. The plus side of this approach is it builds long-term employee loyalty with people who know the business inside and out and at all levels. The downside is very few new ideas are brought to the table from outsiders who have a fresh perspective and haven't been brainwashed on how to do things a certain way. But even if execs are open to bringing in outsiders, the department heads often veto people they think are "smarter" than themselves, who might jeopardize their personal career path or, even worse, innovate the business in a direction that could potentially put their own jobs at risk.

Management: Friend or Foe?

I posed a question on LinkedIn that I didn't realize would evoke such vitriol from people: Is management the enemy of innovation? People said things like:

> Yes, it is. For most managers, their time is short, so instead of forging a path forward, they become risk adverse to line their pockets with fat bonuses. Seen it many times and been victim of it several. If the change is smooth, they take credit. If the change is rough, they throw the change agents under the bus.

> Management is a reflection of what an organization wants. If the CEO professes innovation and pushes people for hard numbers, management cannot be blamed for lack of innovation.

> I pin a whole bunch of this, like others have, on risk aversion, either at the management or exec level, and sometimes from only one (influential) person.

> Bad management, arrogant management, mismanagement and just plain "my way or the highway" type of management stifles morale, productivity, and innovation, and leads to depression, potential abuses

of power, and eventually, good people leaving workplaces that are toxic environments.

If the management team is driven by fear, then yes. Change is scary and spits in the face of what companies want. Companies love stability and by default like to control the playing field. So innovative ideas get dismissed and discounted.

Without management, we wouldn't have business. Companies simply can't scale without process and structure. But many internal cultures take this to the extreme and end up with a command-and-control style, which is definitely what my LinkedIn colleagues experienced. As you go up the chain of command in an organization, people try to squeeze out more inefficiencies and risk. They also look to entrench their place on the corporate ladder and squash any threat that might create a backslide. In fact, research points out that leaders who bring too much creativity to their job may jeopardize their chances for advancement. It's no wonder new ideas shrivel on the vine.

Then there are companies that truly value innovation but can't get their teams to step up to the plate. They've used rewards, incentives, and even trendy hackathons, yet people plod along with the status quo. They've added more diversity to teams and provided physical space and stimulation to help people think outside the box.

And yet, things still don't change.

Great Expectations

Corporate cultures reflect the basic laws of physics: anything at rest will stay at rest, comfortable in its lack of inertia, until a powerful force changes it. Cultures will stick with their status quo stagnation unless a strong, consistent, long-term force creates momentum.

How do you get out of this conundrum? These are the six pillars you must have in place to lead your organization into and through an innovation practice.

1. Innovate on Purpose

Ancient mariners set off from shore with a specific destination in mind. They didn't get on their boats and sail around willy-nilly, seeing what they ran into. Their success hinged on proper navigation. They learned how to steer by the stars for one important reason: When there was nothing else to guide their path, the stars provided an unwavering anchor against which they made decisions. Those decisions led them to destinations that took months or even years to reach. For sailors in the northern hemisphere, the North Star served as their point of reference.

For organizations, purpose serves as that same North Star. And more companies have started to understand the power of purpose as a guide during times of uncertainty. A report from the EY Beacon Institute shares the results of its survey of 1,470 global leaders who represent companies across various industries in developed and emerging markets around the world. The report, *How Can Purpose Reveal a Path Through Disruption?*, explains that purpose, not profit, is the key to success in the midst of a turbulent global economy, particularly as it relates to innovation.

According to the report, 68 percent of the companies that use a broad definition of purpose and infuse it into their organizations say it allows them to innovate when everything's in upheaval. Having a bigger ideal to which to aspire helps keep your employees focused on the long game and ride out the short-term turbulence. This is so important, because when markets fill with uncertainty, the last thing rudderless companies want is add to it by trying to innovate. There are too many unknowns, and executives don't believe they have control over enough of the variables.

The survey also found that 97 percent of companies that deeply integrate a broader sense of purpose say that a good or great deal of incremental value comes from doing so. Whether they're building customer loyalty, making sure they preserve their brand's value and reputation, or encouraging innovation across the company, embedding purpose in everything employees think and do lets companies stay competitive and generates value, even in the toughest economic times.

2. Articulate Values

A brand value is a quality that reflects what an organization believes is important. Being transparent about what your company stands for makes it easy to know if an employee, vendor, consultant, or customer is the right partner. Perpetually innovative companies are that way because they understand how to remove friction. Creating clarity about what you value makes it easy to surround yourself with people who believe what you believe, which makes it easier to accomplish great things.

Take human resources software platform Gusto, for example. CEO Josh Reeves and his two business partners started the company 2012 based on deep empathy for their relatives who worked in small businesses. Values have played a big role in the success, as well as the innovation, of his company.

Gusto offers all-in-one payroll and benefits services to more than 100,000 small- and medium-sized businesses in the United States. They've reimagined payroll, benefits, and human resources for modern companies by automating payroll tax paperwork, so users never have to look at government forms when they file. "Every year in the US you have 40 percent of companies getting fined for incorrectly doing their payroll taxes," Josh explained in a *Forbes* interview.

The company reinforces its brand purpose—helping small businesses take care of their hardworking teams—with six core values:

- **Ownership mentality.** Every employee has the power to make our company better.
- **Don't optimize for the short term.** Short-term gains never justify long-term sacrifice. Invest in the future.
- **We are all builders.** We are collectively building the product and company of our dreams.
- **Go the extra mile.** Go beyond what works. Discover what delights.
- **Do what's right.** What is right isn't the same as what is easy.
- **Be transparent.** Share information. Share mistakes. Share victories.

By 2018, Josh had led the company to a $2 billion market valuation, twice its value from 2015, and a 95 percent user satisfaction rate. When it comes to

advice about how to run an innovative business based on values, he made it
clear in an interview with Y Combinator where he stands:

> Be bold and opinionated with your values, especially when you're
> hiring. You shouldn't have to convince people about your values—
> there's either alignment or not. Surfacing values during interviews and
> having traditions that reflect and reinforce those values is paramount.
> At Gusto, we have core values, and if someone's not a good fit with
> them, it doesn't mean they're a bad person. It just means that they
> could probably do better work somewhere else.

3. Create Space

Space comes in all sorts of forms.

There's the physical space. Open-office plans have been all the rage for the
last decade. Some people love them because it makes collaboration a cinch.
Other hate 'em because they're filled with constant noise and distractions. I'm
certainly not going to suggest you start knocking down walls (or putting them
up) to make way for greater innovation. But have a mix of three types of real
estate so you have flexibility for what you need for different kinds of collaboration (between teams and internal to teams), personalities (introverts and
extroverts), and business needs (employee growth and shrinkage).

Then there's the emotional space. Some people do better if they work by
themselves rather than in a group. When you get people together, the dynamic
can mean some people get talked over and great ideas never get shared. There's
always those who dominate the conversation and others keep mum, so they
don't look ridiculous. To fix this, give people time to think on their own before
coming to group meetings or brainstorming session. Or, give them one-on-one
time to flesh things out with you.

Creating space also means room to fail. Innovation is about trying new
things and seeing what happens. It's common sense that if you truly believe
this is what it's about, then not everything will succeed. When you create
space for people to experiment, push their curiosity, and make incremental
bets, ideas flourish. The more things you try, the more likely you are to find
something that works.

4. Allocate Resources

Innovation in an investment in the future of your business, not an everyday expense. If you believe in it, you'll show it by committing resources to it.

Resources may include giving people dedicated time to work on side projects related to their work. Financial software company Intuit created Bullet Time, sanctioned periods each week for employees to come up with ideas and collaborate. This time was key for Olya Kenney, a user experience specialist, to work on her idea for the Empathy Generator, a virtual reality tool that gave her team members the experience of having the low- to no-vision disabilities for which they were trying to innovate solutions.

Examples of other resources that matter include a space to work, financial support, and access to other Citizen Innovators who can help the chances of success and training. At PayPal, once a year departments have a chance to show off their innovation chops at an internal trade show. It gets employees excited about their ideas, builds support and an internal community around them, and breaks down silos that could rear their head later when it's time to implement ideas.

5. Empower People

Empowering employees is one of the secrets behind door number 3 to make your company more agile. People don't like to be micromanaged, and it has a harsh effect on the bottom line. When you don't give the workers closest to decisions the leeway and authority to find answers, your organization's hierarchy makes decision-making a bottleneck. People waste time hung up waiting as leaders debate, rehash, and compromise with each other. In the meantime, employees get frustrated and customers get impatient. A company's ability to innovate, adapt, and pivot quickly decides its survival. Empowering employees is how you do all of this successfully.

This isn't to say it's easy. Empowering employees with decisions that make room for everyday innovation means you have to shift how you think about things. You have to train them, give them the tools they need, loosen the reins, and get out of their way.

6. Give and Get Feedback

Great innovation requires a high-trust work culture. But most managers and people of position have fragile egos. Research from the *Academy of Management Journal* shows that when managers are insecure, they don't actively look for new ideas and get defensive when people make suggestions. Employees see this and then don't speak up to avoid a career-limiting move. If managers want to show they practice what they preach, they need to openly model it for other people to witness. When employees see that their supervisor is willing to hear criticism and no one's head rolls, they're more likely to speak up.

When a company's too rigid, it's hard for leaders to build an innovative culture and decisions turn into the Gladiator Effect. Research from IE Business School, however, shows that cognitive diversity makes a group smarter. Two heads, it turns out, actually are better than one if we can train people to give and receive feedback in the right way. For leaders, understanding the dynamics of each Citizen Innovator is important so you can create an environment that's better educated on how to ask for and give feedback.

You're the Only One

The difference between being an executive in your company and being a team leader or individual contributor is that you have much more control over culture than anyone else. You don't just react to the culture or adjust it from within; you actually *get to create and lead it*. What you tell people to do as instruction and what you actually do as an example becomes infinitely more powerful. You can do it fully. Team leaders can do it partially. And individual employees can't do it at all.

If you're the CEO, you get to decide the constraints of the company. The business isn't as innovative as you'd like, you say? You have the power to change these things about the company. Because you can do that, and because you're the only one who can, if it is going to be, it has to start with you. Not only do you have the ability to make it happen; you have the responsibility.

When you rethink your approach to innovation, you'll see that great ideas are the responsibility of everyone, not just an island of individuals. As a leader, you have to manage as if you consistently expect new, great, and reliable ideas from everyone, not just the lone geniuses in your organizations. If your culture only makes room for a few people here and there to learn and use the Perpetual Innovation Process, you'll never realize the true potential of your growth, nimbleness, and customer loyalty.

Ideas for Action

1. Innovation Tournaments and Hackathons

ParkMobile rallied its employees by hosting an innovation tournament and encouraging every employee to join in. Other companies go through the same process with customers and some a blend of both. Referred to as crowdsourcing, when you expand participation to front-line employees, you include people who have an intimate understanding of customers' needs that executives never know about. Adding in the perspective of customers means you're co-creating your brand's experience with the ultimate user: the people who fork over money to do business with you. Granted, when you swing the doors open to include these two key groups, it can make you feel really vulnerable. You'll probably hear a slew of things you'd rather not. But the point of innovation tournaments is to increase the number and quality of ideas that impact the efficiency of your company and increase the quality of both what you sell and how you deliver it. I guarantee that the conversations you have along the way will make everyone smarter.

Some companies spread the process out over time, like ParkMobile did for a week, or as supported side projects. Others concentrate them into an intense 24-hour period, which is called a hackathon. While hackathons have the perception of being IT-related, in reality they can be used for any innovative problem-solving situation. With both approaches, the intention is to strengthen the community of people involved, welcome newbies, give people a chance to learn something new, and create space and time for the people involved to make headway on something they're interested in.

Creating contests helps leaders understand who's willing to be a part of innovation even in small ways. An annual innovation tournament at Dow Chemical looks at how to cut back on waste and save energy. The constraints are a budget of no more than $200,000, and the costs have to be recouped within a year. Over the course of a decade, employees came up with 575 projects that have an average return of 204 percent and saved the company $110 million a year.

Download how-to guides for innovation tournaments and hackathons at www.carlajohnson.co/rethinktools.

2. Kill the Company

Shazam co-founder Chris Barton explained how he came up with the idea for the music identification app that he and his partners later sold to Apple for $400 million in 2017.

While living in London during his internship as part of his MBA program, he and his BFFs (and fellow co-founders) Dhiraj Mukherjee and Philip Inghelbrecht came up with the idea for a software product. Chris was frustrated that he couldn't recognize songs on the radio. The team figured they could sell software to radio stations so DJs could keep track of the music they played. Then, the company's software could collect the information in real time and tell users what songs were being played on what stations.

What rocketed the sophistication of the app is when one of Chris's professors from his MBA program asked a crucial question: What could put you out of business? He knew he was onto something.

"What might a competitor be able to do to compete with me once I had this software installed in radio stations across the country and once users were delighted by being able to find out which songs they were playing on the radio?" Chris thought. "What risk was there of someone trumping me or circumventing me? What if someone could identify the song using the actual sound of the music captured over the mobile phone? Then, they would not need to know what the radio station was playing at all because they would actually identify using the sound of the music itself."

This ability to think ahead and think like a potential competitor is what drove big innovation throughout Shazam's little start-up. Once they created the algorithm, they realized that their technology was so much more than just one that recognized music. Their original pitch to investors painted a picture of how people would be able to use the app to not just identify music, but also buy it, watch videos, see lyrics, send greeting cards to friends, find out which songs friends tagged, organize music into playlists, and more features that ultimately made their way into the app.

Shazam changed the music industry by making it easy to find out the name of a new favorite song or artist. But it also gave record labels an early detection system about new potential hit artists, helped artists figure out tour locations based on fan base, and created an alternative place to build audiences.

These savvy innovators knew something that's been a horrifying wake up call for other companies, icons such as Borders bookstores, Palm and its PDAs, and RadioShack. As crazy as it may seem, you have to think about what could put you out of business, then innovate in that direction. Because if you don't, someone else will.

3. Ban the Bloat

Meetings are inevitable. But bad meetings aren't.

One of the biggest things that kills innovation momentum in any organization is meetings inflated with people who don't need to be a part of them. They eat up everyone's time, create bureaucracy, bog down decisions, and suck the creative heart and soul out of ideas. The fewer people you involve, the faster work and ideas happen. Jeff Bezos talks about it in terms of the two-pizza rule: Never have a meeting that's so big that you can't feed all the participants with just two pizzas.

I had a friend who worked at Nordstrom. His boss gave everyone permission to decline a meeting if they didn't feel they'd either contribute to or gain from it. This had a fascinating effect. Those calling meetings then had to become more deliberate and intentional with getting people together. Meetings started having agendas and goals for outcomes. That led to people prepping ahead of time, because the agenda pointed out who was expected to contribute what and why. Others saw they needed to be ready to respond on their part. It was on the shoulders of the person calling the meeting to get others to agree to be there, because the default was to decline. Then, as the length of meetings and the number of people involved went down, the quality of meetings went way up. Instead of rambling two-hour get-togethers, they turned into highly efficient 30-minute sessions.

4. Give People a Voice

Suggestion boxes are the butt of many a corporate joke. Instead of cobweb-infested containers where nothing sees the light of day, they can actually be helpful and rally ideas from people you normally wouldn't hear from. If you have an employee population that works outside of a traditional office environment, this may be a great option. Think about people who work in construction sites, healthcare, postal service, transportation, and other types of professions. Nothing says your suggestion box has to be a physical receptacle. You can create one that's digital, and people can submit their ideas through a website or an app on their phone.

A Dutch steel company used this approach for 70 years, and its 11,000 employees collected an average of 8,500 suggestions annually. An average employee made six or seven suggestions a year, and the company adopted three or four. One particularly prolific employee sent in 75 ideas, and management adopted 30 of them. These little ideas added up to big gains, saving more than $750,000 in a single year.

Getting ideas is half the battle. Next you need to give proof that something actually happens to the ideas people submit. An innovation survey from Accenture found that 72 percent of companies let innovative ideas wither and dies because there's no formal process to review and evaluate what people suggest. Make sure you have an efficient process in place to audit ideas, report back the number of ideas employees submit and what happens next. Then, create a reward system for the ones you implement. This way, employees don't feel their suggestions are all for naught. Download a template for your suggestion box at www.carlajohnson.co/rethinktools.

CHAPTER 13

Getting to Extraordinary Outcomes

W e're in a time in business in which the work you do *must* create an impact. On an individual level, your innovative ideas may be the deciding factor between keeping your job or getting laid off. From a team perspective, it could mean the difference between cutting budgets and getting spread thin, and getting more funding to invest in your project and the skills of your people. At a company level, it can be the differentiator between surviving during a time of crisis and being able to reassure employees, customers, and shareholders that your strategy holds strong and you'll remain in growth mode regardless of what the universe throws at you.

There's always a reason not to innovate. When times are good, no one wants to risk rocking the boat by trying something new. When times are bad, companies focus on cutting every expense possible and telling employees to keep their nose to the grindstone. Productivity and output matter most.

The year 2020 found people around the world in the startling grip of an unprecedented health crisis. COVID-19 was first and foremost a human tragedy that affected millions, whether that was as a patient, a family member, a healthcare professional, or someone whose livelihood depended on either earning a wage or a wage earner. Our need to socially distance moved us from corner offices and cubicles to kitchen tables as we learned to work from home. At the same time, police violence triggered protests calling for governmental, corporate, and cultural change to end racism. It's too early to understand what impact COVID-19 and the Black Lives Matter protests will have on organizations; it will take years—perhaps decades—before we have the emotional space that will bring the perspective we need to properly reflect on this time in history. No person or business of any size or any industry will come away unaffected.

The companies that will rebound the fastest and the highest are the ones that have innovation at the heart of their culture. When every employee in an organization raises their hand with new ideas of how to do anything better, it sparks interest, attention, engagement, ideas, and outcomes. You could be just like the woman who worked in the finance department at ParkMobile, see an opportunity to create a more efficient process, do something about it, and help your company reinvest that time and money into something more valuable for the business.

Necessity Is the Mother of Innovation

At its heart, innovation is about solving problems. In 1666, at the height of the bubonic plague, Isaac Newton packed up his books at the University of Cambridge and headed to his family's home in the countryside of England. It was during this time that he came up with the mathematical concepts he needed to explain his philosophies on gravity and optics. Isaac innovated the entire field of mathematics in a time of crisis simply because he needed a way to prove his theories in physics.

Every person, team, and organization has problems that need solving—even more so in the midst of chaos. While you may think that getting innovation going is easier when times are flush, the opposite may actually be true. During disruption, people expect change to happen. They look at the entire system differently, which unfreezes the organization. People know the processes that have always worked are now up in the air, and it makes room for fresh thinking. In turn, this creates a bias toward action, and people come up with more ideas faster, they make decisions quicker, and they get them into play sooner. This leads to extraordinary outcomes—outcomes that save time or money, make money, or create value beyond anything they could have imagined.

The ability to consistently deliver the level of ideas over a long period of time that turn into extraordinary outcomes for your organization is what puts the *perpetual* in the Perpetual Innovation Process. Your dedication to innovation will create your flywheel for success over decades.

The Innovation Path at Emerson

Up until now, the examples I've shared with you have shown how to come up with a single idea that's new, great, and reliable. As you've seen, the people I've talked about used the Perpetual Innovation framework to innovate in a way that's led to extraordinary outcomes—outcomes so exceptional that they've made a phenomenal impact for them, their teams, and their companies.

What, exactly, does Perpetual Innovation look like in the long run? Let's take a look at how Kathy Button Bell, chief marketing officer at Emerson, has maintained her level of quality ideas, innovation, and extraordinary outcomes over more than a 20-year span.

1999: The Beginning

Kathy joined Emerson Electric in 1999 as their first ever chief marketing officer. When the company brought her on board, it had $14.3 billion in revenue and the brand served as an overarching umbrella for 60 autonomous businesses and hundreds of sub-brands. With 117,000 employees around the world, her charge was to inspire and get the engineering organization to appreciate marketing the company, and make it easier for customers to understand and do business with them.

With all of this top of mind, Kathy took a seemingly small step that made a big difference: She told everyone to stop using acronyms and abbreviations from communications at every level of the company. She even made the top 750 executives sign a pledge to stop using acronyms which made her expectations clear:

> I promise I will no longer use acronyms, abbreviations, initials or other forms of short-handing any brand that includes the name Emerson in any conversations, correspondence, presentations or internal documents. No ECT instead of Emerson Climate Technologies or ENPC instead of Emerson Network Power China. Their use undermines the strength of our brand.

This standard helped make communication simpler throughout the company. Surprisingly, the major transgressors weren't just the engineering teams; human resources, finance, and IT groups all tried to abbreviate information into their own siloed language. It wasn't just that it led to poor communication; it was also lazy and supported a tribal behavior for each group.

2000–2002: Becoming the Chief Complexity Reduction Officer

It became clear the lack of any brand architecture not only weakened the brand portfolio but also demonstrated chaos. Most customers didn't realize they were buying multiple products from different companies all owned by Emerson. Six different salespeople might call on a single customer with six different logos on their business cards. Investors felt Emerson wasn't getting companies to work together well enough or fast enough after it acquired new brands.

Emerson was the pinnacle of efficiency and highly disciplined financial management, but it needed to break with its long tradition of allowing highly autonomous companies to manage their brands independently. Solutions development demanded more brand integration and collaboration between businesses and a different culture to support the change. Finally, the internet age was upon them, thrusting their brand chaos to light by showcasing mismatching websites.

With this in mind, Kathy launched a year-long research and design project to create a brand promise, design the brand architecture, and create a fresh new logo. Her agency team interviewed hundreds of executives, employees, customers, and investors to explore the Emerson brand stretch and how they could take advantage of it. They combed through hundreds of pages of competitive data then started to create a strawman of who Emerson could be.

First, they defined the essence of the Emerson culture. "Engineering Full-on" described the force that drove Emerson. The research helped them define the unmatched passion and zeal they had for solving their customers' toughest challenges. This became the backbone for their brand promise: Emerson is where technology and engineering come together to create solutions for the benefit of our customers, driven without compromise for a world in action.

Emerson had always had this zealous personality—aka "full-on"—which the brand promise now reflected. The new stretch for the company was "coming together to create solutions," which touched the untouchable autonomy of the businesses.

The new Emerson brand architecture fell directly from "coming together" and drove the strategy to make the enterprise into eight distinct brand platforms, each under the Emerson name (e.g., Emerson Process Management, Emerson Climate Technologies). This was a dramatic shift from the 60 autonomous and individually branded product companies.

Emerson hadn't changed its logo since 1967. They developed six potential new logos and added 10 top business schools' students to the research. They were unanimous in their choice of a newer, fresher, more modern logo: the Emerson double helix. The blue capital letters were symbolic of its strength and durability, and the silver helix was to represent the individual businesses coming together.

2001: Consider It Solved

Creating the brand promise gave the marketing team a fundamental platform through which they could tell a unified story. It was now time to take the brand promise externally, and Emerson turned to DDB's creative director Marcia Iacobucci (head of the Emerson account since 1997) to develop a look, feel, and personality for Emerson to use in ads to reflect all the brand work that had been done. Paramount in her exploration and design work was creation of an Emerson tagline that could umbrella the entire company's communications. "Emerson Consider It Solved" was born on the last frame of some television advertising concept boards in 2001. It was love at first sight both for Kathy and Dave Farr, (CEO of Emerson) as well as the other Emerson leaders. But it has stood the test of time and remains on ads from the entire company to this day. It reflects what Emerson zealously does every day for its customers and is considered more than just a tagline. It's the ethos and core brand idea for the company. It's what the company does, not what it makes.

Emerson's "Consider It Solved" brand promise underscores
the company's entire communications message.

2005: Research and Innovation

In looking at how the company solved problems for customers and the industry, executives uncovered a major realization: A lot of the work that the product development team did wasn't actually new and innovative; it was just product revisions (otherwise known as cost reductions). Whether major or minor ones, they helped protect profit and market share for Emerson.

"This approach really just cuts costs," Kathy explained, "but sooner or later you use up all your running room. You can't shrink to success, and you have to invest in future innovation, or you will wither and fail."

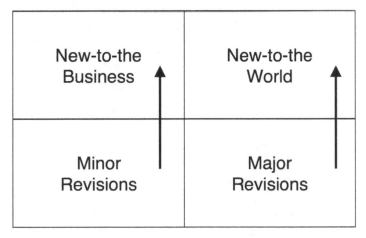

Emerson's approach to innovation shifted from product revisions to truly innovative ideas by tapping into market research and moving resources toward the top of the matrix.

The interesting thing about the bottom row of the chart above is that major and minor revisions deliver very dependable short-term results because there is an established, proven market for what you are selling. They're the kinds of things corporations love. Executives know it's going to work, and they're low risk. Before Emerson could rise to the top level, it had to invest resources. This became a priority as executives realized why new product introductions were underperforming.

When chief technology officer Randall Ledford came up with the innovation framework, it was the wake-up call the company needed. In order to move from a mindset of revisions to new-to-the business or world, Emerson needed to invest in finding out what was most important to customers and the industry. Kathy started where it mattered most for this highly left-brained, engineer-driven organization—research.

"Everything starts with research—what we nicknamed Stage Gate Zero. We took the voice of the customer and backed it up to the beginning of everything we create and deliver."

Stage 1
Market Research
"ZERO"

Stage 2
Idea Generation

Stage 3
Concept Feasibility

Stage 4
Concept Development & Project Planning

Stage 5
Design & Development

Stage 6
Ramp Up

Stage 7
Launch & Production Start-up

Stage 8
Production

"The stickler with many business-to-business companies is they wait until stage five or six—when they've started producing a product—and then show it to customers to hear what they think," Kathy said. "We wanted to instill the voice of our customers into the earliest stages of product development for a more innovative approach. This is because many of the answers to our customers' problems aren't product-focused anymore. For example, they might want a single invoice for a complex bundle of products, software, and solutions. As our customers get savvier, they look for things like efficiency, productivity, and cost savings because financial demands are stringent. If you can make doing business easier for your customers, you're golden."

Once the research and innovation spirit were engrained in the company's culture and customers' minds, Kathy and Marcia Iacobucci, the senior vice president and group creative director at DDB in Chicago, began work on the next chapter—communicating Emerson's innovation model of driving organic growth during a time when the world was reeling from an economic downturn.

2009: Never Been Done Before

This next stage brought a marked change in how the company showed up in the world (see chapter 7). By using the inspiration from the Apple iPod ad, Kathy and Marcia infused bright colors, bold graphics, sound, and clear,

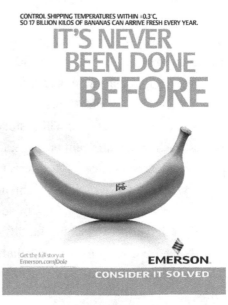

simple messaging into the brand. It positioned Emerson as the "optimistic face of global business" when business was anything but.

The timing was perfect. Through a string of "Never Been Done Before" messages, the company helped customers protect vital infrastructures, find new sources of clean energy, and prevent tons of fresh food from spoiling.

2015: 125th Anniversary Celebration and #WeLoveSTEM

As 2015 approached, Emerson created a tremendous opportunity to pivot the company—celebrating its 125th anniversary. The brand had been steadfast in its successful operations and improved results every year. Over more than a century in business, it established itself as the epitome of consistency, a reliable investment, and secure employer among big businesses, especially manufacturers. That legacy had led to an incredible streak of success—58 straight years (which has now grown to 64) of increased dividends per share creating the reputation as a rare "dividend king." However, as the industry and landscape of business shifted, the company knew it needed to transform to keep that track record going for the next 125 years.

"An inflection point is a great time for creativity, but you have to be aware of them and exploit them. Although '125' felt as awkward as a 37th birthday, the milestone allowed us permission to celebrate the durability of our culture while accelerating change," Kathy said. "The rule of public relations is that the antithesis of expectation gets the headline. This was an opportunity for Emerson to show up differently, so everything we did had to be unexpected. We decided to reverse common thinking and spend 10 percent of the time celebrating our history and 90 percent forward looking."

The celebration started with a storytelling arc that broke into three discrete layers, each with a different purpose, in order to elevate and integrate Emerson and supercharge change: "Celebrate. Challenge. Consider It Solved."

- **Celebrate** was about right now. It gave permission to take a deep breath and enjoy the fun of success—if only for a brief moment.
- **Challenge** was about the difficult opportunities that are always ahead and the edgy excitement that goes with attempting something that's never been done before.

Celebrate. Challenge. Consider It Solved.

	Celebrate	Challenge	Consider It Solved
The time frame	Now	Ahead	Legacy
The feeling	Fun	Edge	Warmth
The substance	10 seconds of joy	Never Been Done Before	Leaving our world in a better place

- **Consider It Solved** was about Emerson's fabulous long legacy and the warmth of those who came before. Emerson employees needed to live up to that legacy and take on the responsibility to leave the company and the world a better place than they found it.

To get Emerson to appear in new, unexpected places, Kathy knew she needed a story bigger than just an anniversary celebration. Emerson CEO David Farr had been frustrated with the lack of college students choosing careers in science, technology, engineering, and math (STEM). This made both of them take a step back for a bigger perspective to understand what challenged Emerson's customers the most—a talent drought. Attracting future talent had become a cause for serious concern. At the time, only 16 percent of America's high school seniors were considered proficient in math and thought about a career in STEM. Of those who went on to start a STEM major in college, 38 percent didn't finish. And even among those who did, only about half ended up going to work in a related field.

He realized that without an infusion of young talent, both Emerson and its customer base would struggle to bring new ideas and innovation to the industry. This 125-year old engineering-driven company saw that it was time to take a deep dive into how it was perceived by engineering graduates wooed by the likes of Netflix, Apple, and other companies more provocative than

Emerson. It also needed to entice more talent into engineering majors and keep them in the profession.

To connect with a younger audience, Kathy looked for someone who could influence an interest in science for a younger generation.

"We talked about Simon Helberg, who played Howard the engineer on *The Big Bang Theory*," Kathy shared, "but he's an actor, not actually involved in science. Whoever we chose had to be the real deal."

Instead, her agency brought her the idea of partnering with internet star Hank Green. A relevant, wildly popular geek-chic celebrity, Hank and his brother started a video blog in 2007 called *Vlogbrothers*. With trendy science videos like *SciShow* and *Crash Course* helping teens pass their AP science and math exams, their YouTube channel has more than 3.3 million subscribers. To test the waters, Kathy asked her high-school-age son what he thought. When he replied that using Hank's videos were how he got a 4.0 on his biology advanced placement test, she knew they'd scored big time.

Leveraging the 125th anniversary celebration to accelerate change, Emerson and Hank launched the brand's #WeLoveSTEM push to inspire and empower the next generation of engineers by connecting science to technology advances and modern conveniences.

Kathy explained: "Emerson's STEM focus influenced the company's marketing and recruiting efforts, and this first-of-its-kind campaign for the company was designed to entertain and inspire current engineers as well as a future generation of businesspeople. Hank brought a sense of humor to the topic that made a big difference. Hank is a lifestyle."

Emerson took an unconventional approach to sharing its message in the media, such as these ads from the *Wall Street Journal*, in order to capture the attention of its target customers and create a buzz.

As part of this campaign, Emerson launched its first-ever national network TV ad—a highly unorthodox tactic in business-to-business marketing—on CBS's *The Big Bang Theory*. Hank served as the ad talent and encouraged young people to visit the "We Love STEM" section of Emerson.com to learn more about different areas of science. *Big Bang Theory* producer Chuck Lorre loved it so much he tweeted, "this was the most relevant commercial that has ever run on our show."

The results of the 125th anniversary and #WeLoveSTEM launches were truly extraordinary.

125th anniversary celebration results:

- Nearly 1 billion impressions brought by more than 20 media interviews for Emerson executives
- 130 stories published in print media
- Top-tier broadcast media placements
- 270 satellite media tour airings (A satellite media tour is when subject-matter experts are available to speak with the media in diverse markets for a specific time period, perhaps one to four hours. Emerson targeted Atlanta, Austin, Columbus, Jacksonville, Milwaukee, Minneapolis, and Philadelphia.)
- 20,708 views of Emerson's "Brief Moment of Joy" video made for the anniversary celebration

#WeLoveSTEM results at the end of the 2015 campaign

- 16.3 million social media impressions
- 2 million page views of #ILoveSTEM website and 1.3 million unique external visits
- 439,000+ views of videos from #ILoveSTEM partnership with Hank Green (shattering the 2014 benchmark of 25,000 views for the same time)
- 439,000 views of STEM-related videos produced by Emerson
- 9.7 percent increase in resume submission through the Emerson.com career page compared with the same period from 2014

2016: Divestiture and Values

Behind the scenes, the company was posed to engineer a significant transformation: selling off $6 billion of business and moving from five distinct businesses to two focused platforms—as seamlessly as possible. And doing this while continuing to respond to increasing customer demand for software and solutions and maintaining the positive financial performance the shareholders expected. Coming off the anniversary celebration was the perfect time to create a single set of values for the company.

Historically, many of the individual businesses had their own, which were a mishmash of ideals, all with a similarly dull vocabulary. Kathy now had the opportunity to define Emerson's purpose in the world as a brand, developing what the executive team referred to as their Noble Causes—how the company leaves the world in a better place. These have replaced the company's traditional mission statement as more practical ways of expressing what employees believe in and how they'll behave.

Emerson's success for the next 125 years hinged on 75,000+ employees—who were still used to working in siloed businesses—coming together across 200 locations worldwide as One Emerson. Kathy and her team quickly realized that aligning the organization around one common set of values would give them a single road map for the new way Emerson would work as a collaborative team, united in common strengths and with shared aspirations for growth. However, it wasn't enough to simply create the values. The team needed to develop a process and opportunities for employees to become an active part in developing them by sharing what drove and inspired them every day.

Kathy's team sent out surveys to a cross section of employees, asking them to share their opinions on questions such as, "What are we best at?" and "What do we need to do more of to be successful?" The 13,999 responses they received (74 percent of those invited) helped define the qualities and beliefs that created the values Emerson uses to fuel its drive to leave the world in a better place than they found it:

1. **Integrity.** We are uncompromising in our honest and ethical behavior, which creates trusting relationships with one another, customers, suppliers, and communities.

2. **Safety & Quality.** We are unwavering in our commitment to the highest standards of safety and quality for ourselves and our customers.

3. **Support Our People**. We attract, develop, and retain exceptional people in an inclusive work environment, where all employees can reach their greatest potential.

4. **Customer Focus.** We actively listen to our customers to deeply understand their needs and deliver the unique solutions that ensure their success.

Emerson Transformation Reflected Through Storytelling

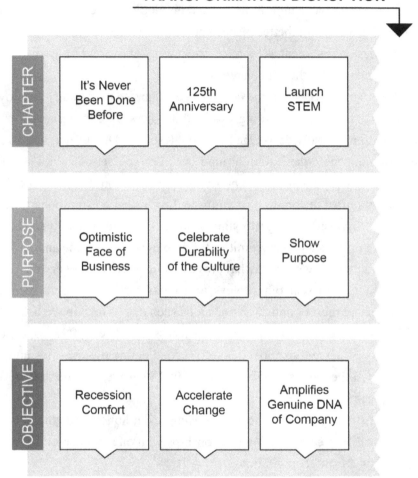

TRANSFORMATION DISRUPTION

CHAPTER
- It's Never Been Done Before
- 125th Anniversary
- Launch STEM

PURPOSE
- Optimistic Face of Business
- Celebrate Durability of the Culture
- Show Purpose

OBJECTIVE
- Recession Comfort
- Accelerate Change
- Amplifies Genuine DNA of Company

5. **Continuous Improvement.** We constantly strive for improvement in all aspects of our business, guided by metrics, feedback, and our disciplined management process.

6. **Collaboration.** We work seamlessly across geographies, platforms, business units, and functions to fully leverage our unmatched breadth and expertise.

Emerson chief marketing officer Kathy Button Bell carefully architected the brand's story over more than two decades to usher in change and a unified culture, both of which fuel employees' outlook on innovation.

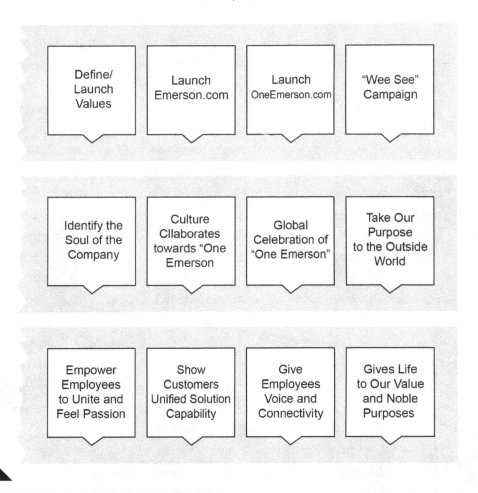

Define/ Launch Values	Launch Emerson.com	Launch OneEmerson.com	"Wee See" Campaign
Identify the Soul of the Company	Culture Cllaborates towards "One Emerson	Global Celebration of "One Emerson"	Take Our Purpose to the Outside World
Empower Employees to Unite and Feel Passion	Show Customers Unified Solution Capability	Give Employees Voice and Connectivity	Gives Life to Our Value and Noble Purposes

DEFINE NOBLE CAUSES

7. **Innovation.** We passionately pursue new technologies, capabilities, and approaches to drive tangible value for our customers.

Once the values were identified, marketing worked with human resources to pioneer an unprecedented, cross-functional global taskforce to organize a five-month launch of activities that cascaded the values to employees worldwide. The message of unified values was delivered in more than 33 languages during in-person meetings and reinforced by using a variety of approaches. For example, Emerson orchestrated a campus takeover at its St. Louis head-quarters by hanging banners on light poles, in lobbies, and in hallways to introduce the new values with colorful and eye-popping pictures.

When it came time for a video to announce the values, Kathy again took inspiration from the unexpected: Barbie. That's right, Barbie. Kathy had come across a TV commercial that the toy maker produced celebrating father-daughter relationships called "Dads Who Play Barbie." The unexpected twist of dads playing Barbie with their daughters showed the power of an authentic moment. That insight was the catalyst for using children to show the unscripted truth of Emerson's values.

Using children to explain Emerson's values was an ingenious approach to break through the logically inclined engineering culture and introduce them in a meaningful way. And there were no better children than those of Emerson employees to tell the story. In interviewing 78 children in multiple facilities about their parents' jobs, family beliefs, and what they thought the Emerson values meant, the team created an emotional connection to them while bringing a sense of truth, authenticity, and warmth to everyone.

The impact of the first-of-its-kind approach that Emerson took to launch its values showed in its ability to create a movement within the organization. The marketing team received more than 280 requests for large marquee values signs to display in lobbies and other public office areas worldwide. In just the first three months, the marketing team had:
- 11 language requests for values posters and video translations
- 33 language requests for full values framework translations
- More than 1,025 value poster sets requested and shipped globally
- 15,836 page views by 1,133 returning visitors to the dedicated OneEmerson.com hub
- Perhaps even more importantly, 4,530 new visitors spent an average of 2.64 minutes per page

"The Barbie ad sticks because there's a shine to the kids and a truth to the message. That's hard to bring into the corporate culture. It's the juxtaposition that worked inside our company—the unexpectedness of having children explain values to an engineering culture."

As if this weren't enough of an undertaking, the next step was to take Emerson's Noble Causes to external audiences from shareholders to customers. The intention was to reorient how the company talked about itself, shifting from focusing on its technology accomplishment for customers to rising to what it could do for industry and what the world needs.

A shift from…	To…
Focusing on our innovation	Focusing on our role in the world
What customers need	What the world needs
Doing many incredible things	Rising to the new challenges we collectively face

"We asked our customers to look more closely at the issues and see what we see—the possibilities," said Kathy. Using elements that created an experience, the campaign involved wrapping columns in major airports such as Chicago's O'Hare and Houston's George Bush Intercontinental Airport with "We See…" stories about the company's problem-solving innovation.

The campaign shattered Emerson's awareness and engagement benchmarks. When surveying customers, people responding that Emerson's "brand favorability" improved by 35 percent with the company's target audience, and the number who said that it "keeps pace with emerging technologies" went up 24 percent. Next, Kathy focused on increasing awareness and consideration in important global and technical markets, such as China, Germany, and Saudi Arabia.

Through 20 years of consistently new, great, and reliable ideas, Kathy has had the same approach as a Perpetual Innovator.

"You have to constantly look for inspiration from the world around you. You have to make sure you're always relevant, showing up in the places people expect you to, but always in unexpected ways. We've 'younged up' the way we present all of our messages to both employees and customers. We have music from alternative bands in our ads. We create infographics and YouTube content. We're also creating many more smart phone videos. Every day we keep getting more authentic and fun.

"Company values and noble causes shape and define an organization during difficult times and days of deep transformation. I look at Emerson and feel that it is an entire culture of innovation. We really have created Citizen Innovators at all levels, not just people on the senior team. Everyone's expected to behave like this.

"You can change the story that a company tells about itself, but you have to do it slowly. It felt like we turned the *Queen Mary* in a bathtub with our brand architecture 20 years ago. Since then, we've stretched Emerson as much as we can stretch it every minute of every day, every year. We did that by giving people values, giving them purpose, giving them a road map, and giving them something to believe in that's bigger than themselves."

CHAPTER 14

Conclusion

Throughout his 92 years, Pablo Picasso produced about 147,800 pieces of work, made up of paintings, prints, engravings, sculptures, ceramics, and illustrations. The *Guinness Book of World Records* lists him as the most prolific painter of all time.

I've studied Pablo and his work for many years, and he may be the ultimate master when it comes to Perpetual Innovation. His work follows the same framework of finding inspiration in the world around him, making sense of it, connecting it to his own work in whatever format that was, and then generating ideas—*lots* of ideas—that led to extraordinary outcomes not only for himself, but for the artworld. By observing works from Paul Cézanne, Henri Rousseau, and archaic and tribal art, he came up with ideas that turned into cubism. He later morphed cubism into collage. He blended high art with popular culture. World events evolved into neoclassicism and surrealism pieces. Pablo went on to influence some of the most iconic artists of the 20th century, such as Jackson Pollock, David Hockney, and Jasper Johns.

Pablo was a master at rethinking the work that he did. As a Perpetual Innovator, he understood that it was all about forward movement. Like the art that he produced, innovation is a journey that ever evolves.

This intent on moving forward is true for each of the people you've learned from in this book.

Carey Smith took inspiration from a sandwich deli in Ann Arbor, Michigan, to build a foundation for Big Ass Fans. The company executed it so well that in 2017 he sold it to private equity firm Lindsay Goldberg. Now, Carey splits his time between Austin, New York City, and Lexington as he runs his new business, a venture capital firm called Unorthodox Ventures. "Everything is about building," Carey explained. "You should always get better. The next thing is always better than the last thing." His ultimate goal with his new quest? To bring his contrarian point of view to entrepreneurs to help them scale their business in half the time.

Comedian Tim Washer put his career at Cisco in the rearview mirror. Since 2017, he's transitioned into working for himself and producing comedy for brands. For example, he worked with the Infogix team to create a video explaining data governance from the cost-benefit analysis of a squirrel considering whether or not it should cross the street. Writing and producing these types of projects are a small part of the work he does through his company, Ridiculous Media. Tim's biggest endeavor is teaching people and teams to use the rules of improv to create possibility-seeking, risk-tolerant cultures. He's also a popular speaker and event emcee. His dry wit is perfect for keeping the energy up during events and drawing out the personality of executives. And last, he's working on a comedy series to pitch to Netflix.

Dave Daigle's ability to rally people's interest in 2011 for disaster preparedness through the story of a zombie apocalypse still captures the public's attention. A decade later, people continue to reach out to Dave asking him about the campaign, reminiscing how it helped them prepare for a zombie apocalypse, and inevitably requesting more of his content. It's been a cornerstone example for communicators about what's possible when you tap into the right inspiration to generate new ideas.

When it comes to Ben Bacal, the ideas keep flowing. He launched Rila Mobile, a software platform dubbed "the Instagram of real estate." The software reverses the typical listing and buyer-seller relationship by crowd-sourcing listings while encouraging engagement, networking, and lifestyle matching. He remains one of the top real estate agents in the country and opened his own brand, Revel Real Estate, in late 2019. He's flipped the traditional office model in that he welcomes his agents to develop a strong personal brand. Ben's intention is to back them up with a full-service technology and marketing platform. He knows that a real estate agent who's truly innovative also has to be tech savvy.

Ben Kohlmann left the Navy in 2018 to follow his heart and pursue an entrepreneurial path that gave him a chance to strengthen his innovation chops. He now works as an engagement manager at McKinsey & Company, setting up and rolling out innovation programs for his clients. While he had plenty of practice leading teams and teaching people how to come up with new, great, and reliable ideas and then bring them to market while in the Navy, he says the freedom he's been given working with clients in his current role has been his most powerful lesson in innovation. A random outcome of Ben's innovation efforts is his podcast, *A Random Walk with Ben Kohlmann*. He uses it to dig into his deep intellectual curiosity on diverse topics with voices from every corner of creation, which supports his belief of how innovation happens— bringing together nonintuitive ideas to create aha moments that people never saw before seemingly separate topics collided.

As for Jeff Perkins, ParkMobile has hosted two more Innovation Weeks and plans to continue them about every six months. They've moved beyond just a parking app and now partner with urban areas and city planners to create a technology platform that consolidates all of the parking payment systems and understands the demand and planning for future parking.

"We're about parking, but also about helping people get smart with mobility," Jeff explained. "We're looking at putting in sensors so people can look at our app and see red and green zones. Other companies feed data into our system that give our customers a much bigger picture." For 2020, they moved into a prepaid service and making reservations at venues for event parking.

Each of these people, along with Kathy Button Bell and Marcia Iacobucci, show the impact of someone who accepts their full potential as a Perpetual Innovator. Each of them proved their ability to move beyond a one-and-done mentality and consistently, over long periods of time, delivered the new, great, and reliable ideas that turned into extraordinary outcomes. They've learned that this is the key to responding to customer requests when asked and being able to invoke hardcore pivots when needed.

Each of them has learned to not only rethink innovation, what it looks like, and the role they have in it, but they also have upped the ante in what they believe they can impact.

Now that you have learned the Perpetual Innovation framework, you know how to consistently come up with new, great, and reliable ideas. You also understand why it's important to focus on innovation at every level of an organization—individually through Citizen Innovators, together through teams, and also through a strong, cohesive culture that makes room for innovation and rewards it.

My question for you now is this: How will you begin to rethink innovation? What will you do differently?

Your innovation story is what you make of it. You have everything in your hand that *you* need to become a Perpetual Innovator. What does your story look like, not just for the next few ideas you need to come up with, but for the next 20 years of your career?

Now's *your* time to rethink the work that you do and the impact you can have.

Make it extraordinary.

About the Author

Photo credit: January Johnson

Carla Johnson is a world-renowned storyteller, an entertaining speaker, and a prolific author.

Having lived, worked, and keynoted on five continents, she's partnered with top brands and conferences to train thousands of people how to rethink the work that they do and the impact they can have. Her visionary expertise has inspired and equipped leaders at all levels to embrace change, welcome new ideas, and transform their business.

Carla plans to change the way we think about innovation—who's invited to the table, what's involved, and how ideas come to life. Her goal is to teach one million people how to become innovators by 2025 so the world is fueled with more diverse ideas that solve complex problems and create a better quality of life for everyone, everywhere.

The author of nine other books, Carla lives in Denver, Colorado, with her husband, Ron; three children, Melinda, Abby, and Nick; two parakeets; and a 15-pound terrier named Max.

Acknowledgments

You're mad, bonkers, completely off your head.
But I'll tell you a secret.
All the best people are.

                                       —Alice in *Alice in Wonderland*

I've had the privilege of many teachers on the journey of this book. Their unconventional thinking has broadened my own. They've taught me to look at the world differently. And their generosity is nothing short of humbling.

I'd like to thank Andrew Davis, who helped me discover the little seed that turned into the big idea for this book. Through color wheels, bow ties, and innovation factories, your nonstop energy and curiosity were the dominant force that challenged me to constantly dig deeper and look for the universal message. There's no one who knows how to rethink the world around us like you do and make it a heckuva good time in the process.

Kathy Button Bell, I am indebted to you for sharing every aspect of your creative strategies, innovation prowess, and political expertise for me to learn from. You are not only the vortex of fun, you are the heart and soul who inspires everyone to go beyond what they believe possible—especially me.

To Bryan Kramer, who continually pointed out that nothing extraordinary ever happens without the human element. You reminded me to shine the light on the most important area of innovation—the people.

For the overall structure and narrative, I'd to thank my editor, James Ranson. You truly have a gift for bringing out the story that needed to be told. You made everything about this book bigger and tremendously better than it would have been without you. I'm ever grateful to Book Launchers and Julie Broad for bringing us together.

The talented Marcie Hancock, Joseph Kalanowski, and Jan Zlotnick brought to life the book cover and interior images. All of you are are amazing at taking the randomness in my head and making it look amazing in the real world.

To those who talked through my early ideas and processes, thank you for your insights and candor in helping me point the theme for this book in the right direction: Dr. Karen Bartuch, Michael Brenner, Eduardo Conrado, Robin Doerr, Marcia Iacobucci, and Tom Stein.

It takes quite a few hands to bring a book to life, not to mention to market. Thank you, Julie Broad at Book Launchers, for guiding me through the early stages of structure and development. Lori Paximadis, as a copyeditor and proofreader, you're the true guardian of the English language. Thank you for being excellent with every detail.

I deeply appreciate the confidence that David Hancock had in me as a first-time author with Morgan James Publishing. You and your team are exceptional not only at giving a message a bigger platform, but at making the entire process along the way collaborative, rewarding, purposeful, and downright fun.

Thank you to the many extraordinary people who guided me along the way, supported my work, shared their insights, challenged me on what I believed, and let me share their story. This work belongs to all of us: Brian Solis (for writing the foreword), Howard Behar, José Berengueres, Allison Canty, Dorie Clark, Dave Daigle, the Fast Forward Forum community, Cindy Gallop, Amisha Gandhi, Sunnie Groeneveld, Jeremy Gutsche, Jeremy Harrison, Toni

Clayton-Hine, Joseph Jaffe, Lorin Kaufman, Ben Kohlmann, Doug Kessler, Courtney Smith Kramer, Rebecca Lieb, Tamara McCleary, Dhiraj Mukherjee, Brian Moran, Evelyn Neil, Laura Gassner Otting, Jeremiah Owyang, Jeff Perkins, José Pires, Jim Roberts, Saga Shoffner, Carey Smith, Teresa Taylor, Tim Washer, and Trish Witkowski.

To my mother, thank you for teaching me to think, and rethink, for myself. Your insistence that I become a student of the world at an early age set me on a life path I never imagined would become so meaningful. You will forever be the example of kindness, compassion, and love I hope to emulate.

This is the 10th book I've written or coauthored. It takes a lot of sacrifice, not only from me but from the people nearest and dearest to me, my family. Thank you, Ron, Mel, Abby, and Nick, for the support you've given while I researched and wrote this book. You've had never-ending patience while I picked apart your own idea-generation processes, humored me as I tested frameworks on you, and let me bend your ear about creativity, innovation, and corporate culture to the point that each of you could have written your own version of this book. You make me proud and eternally grateful.

Notes

Chapter 1: What Is Innovation?

McKinsey & Company: McKinsey & Company, Growth & Innovation. Accessed September 9, 2019. https://www.mckinsey.com/business-functions/strategy-and-corporate-finance/how-we-help-clients/growth-and-innovation

Fast Company: Todhunter, James. "Defining Innovation." *Fast Company.* April 22, 2009. Accessed September 9, 2019. https://www.fastcompany.com/1273187/defining-innovation

George Damis Yancopoulos: "Why Innovation is Tough to Define—and Even Tougher to Cultivate." *Knowledge@Wharton.* April 13, 2013. Accessed September 9, 2019. https://knowledge.wharton.upenn.edu/article/why-innovation-is-tough-to-define-and-even-tougher-to-cultivate

Department of Industry, Australian government: Department of Industry, Innovation and Science, Australian Government website. Accessed September 9, 2019. https://www.business.gov.au/change-and-growth/innovation

Gijs van Wulfen: Skillicorn, Nick. *What Is Innovation? 15 Innovation Experts Give Us Their Definition.* Idea to Value. March 18, 2016. Accessed September 9, 2019. https://www.ideatovalue.com/inno/nickskillicorn/2016/03/innovation-15-experts-share-innovation-definition

Part 1: How to Innovate: The Perpetual Innovation Process

"We had one phone": Carey Smith, interview with the author, January 18, 2017, and May 5, 2020. Carey described the experience he had while a customer at Zingerman's Deli and how that experience inspired and influenced how he established his branding and made quality a pillar of the company's reputation.

Chapter 3: Setting Objectives

Washer received a request…: Tim Washer, interview with the author, January 18, 2017, and January 8, 2020.

Chapter 4: Step 1—Observe: Collecting Dots

the response: zombies: Kruvand, M., and M. Silver. "Zombies Gone Viral: How a Fictional Zombie Invasion Helped CDC Promote Emergency Preparedness. *Case Studies in Strategic Communication 2* (2013). Accessed February 3, 2020. http://cssc.uscannenberg.org/cases/v2/v2art3. Unless otherwise noted, information about this campaign comes from this article.

the team felt it was worth a try: Dave Daigle, interview with the author, February 6, 2020. He described the atmosphere for innovation in his department at the CDC. He and his team hoped to create influence with adults by making inroads with children, and then have the children put pressure on parents to make preparations for emergencies.

was a trending topic on Twitter: Marsh, Wendell, and Greg McCune. "CDC 'Zombie Apocalypse' Disaster Campaign Crashes Website." *Reuters*. May 19, 2011. Accessed February 5, 2020. https://www.reuters.com/article/us-zombies/cdc-zombie-apocalypse-disaster-campaign-crashes-website-idUSTRE74I7H420110519

cost a total of $87: Dave Daigle, interview with the author, February 6, 2020.

Chapter 7: Step 4—Generate: Becoming an Idea Factory

"Business was stressful": Kathy Button Bell, interview with the author, March 14, 2017. Kathy Button Bell provided a full backstory of the economic environment in which she needed to find new inspiration for her campaign, the financial environment, and the process she and her team used to execute the idea.

"We were able to take Kathy's inspiration": Marcia Iacobucci, interview with the author, January 10, 2017.

the campaign improved confidence: Kathy Button Bell, interview with the author, March 14, 2017.

Chapter 8: Step 5—Pitch: Creating an Idea Journey

"The most innovative corporate environments": Andrew Davis, interview with the author, May 13, 2019.

Chapter 9: Creating a Culture of Original Thinkers

the ones who pushed back against authority: Ben Kohlmann, interview with the author, February 5, 2020. Ben Kohlmann information and quotes throughout the rest of this chapter from this interview unless otherwise noted.

3D printers on ships. Grant, Adam. "How to Build a Culture of Originality."

GhostSwimmer fish robot. Myers, Meghann. "Rising Innovation Star Knocks Navy's Career Rigidity." *Navy Times.* August 31, 2015. Accessed December 19, 2019. https://www.navytimes.com/news/your-navy/2015/08/31/rising-innovation-star-knocks-navy-s-career-rigidity

"When people discovered their voice": Grant, Adam. "How to Build a Culture of Originality."

Chapter 10: Innovation at the Individual Level

"We're the place where dreams go to die": Michael Brenner, interview with the author, May 13, 2019.

Chapter 11: Innovation at the Team Level

20 percent jump in just one quarter: "Interview with an Innovator—Episode 1 with Michael Brenner on Why Mean People Suck." October 24, 2019. Accessed October 24, 2019. https://www.youtube.com/watch?v=co_NcuwTW0g

Chapter 12: Innovation at the Corporate Level

"In many businesses...": Jeff Perkins, interviews with the author, April 17, 2019, and January 14, 2020. Jeff Perkins's information and quotes throughout the rest of this chapter are from this interview.

Chapter 13: Getting to Extraordinary Outcomes

Kathy Button Bell: Kathy Button Bell interviews, 2017, 2018, 2020. Marcia Iacobucci interview, 2017. The events, details, and metrics for the Emerson story come from interviews with Kathy Button Bell, Marcia Iacobucci, and internal documents provided by them to the author.

Chapter 14: Conclusion

"Everything is about building": Carey Smith (2017, 2020).
comedian Tim Washer: Tim Washer, interview with the author, March 5, 2020.
Dave Daigle's ability: Dave Daigle (2020).
A Random Walk with Ben Kohlmann: Ben Kohlmann, interview with the author, June 18, 2020.
moving into a prepaid service: Jeff Perkins, interview with the author, January 14, 2020.

CPSIA information can be obtained
at www.ICGtesting.com
Printed in the USA
JSHW032201180321
12591JS00002B/6

9 781631 953170